# TIME and MYTH

*By the same author*

THE CITY OF THE GODS

A SEARCH FOR GOD IN TIME AND MEMORY

THE WAY OF ALL THE EARTH

# TIME and MYTH

John S. Dunne

UNIVERSITY OF NOTRE DAME PRESS
NOTRE DAME                    LONDON

University of Notre Dame Press edition 1975


Copyright © 1973 John S. Dunne


First edition 1973 by Doubleday & Company, Inc.
Published by arrangement with Doubleday & Company, Inc.
Printed in the United States of America




Second Printing   1976
Third Printing    1978
Fourth Printing   1980
Fifth Printing    1983




Library of Congress Cataloging in Publication Data

Dunne, John S    1929–
    Time and myth.

    Reprint of the ed. published by Doubleday, New York.
    Based on the Thomas More Lectures delivered at
Yale, Feb. 1971.
    Includes bibliographical references.
    1. Life.  2. Death.  I. Title.
[BD431.D846 1975]   128'.5        74-32289
ISBN 0-268-01828-6

# Contents

# Acknowledgments

I would like to thank Father Richard Russell and the Thomas More Foundation for inviting me to give the Thomas More Lectures at Yale in February 1971. This book is based on those lectures, though each lecture has been greatly transformed in the writing.

# TIME and MYTH

# Preface

What kind of story are we in? Is it the story of an adventure, a journey, a voyage of discovery? Or is it something simpler like the story of a child playing by the sea? "I do not know what I may appear to the world," Isaac Newton said in his old age, "but to myself I seem to have been only like a boy playing on the seashore, and diverting myself in now and then finding a smoother pebble or a prettier shell than ordinary, whilst the great ocean of truth lay all undiscovered before me."[1]

If we are in the story of an adventure, a journey, a voyage of discovery, we are in a story where time is all important. Our journey may in fact be a quest of life like that of Gilgamesh, carrying us to the boundaries of life in an effort to conquer death. Or it may be a return from the boundaries, a journey like that of Odysseus, carrying us from the wonderland of death back into the life that can be lived within the boundaries set for us by time. It may be like a journey through the otherworld, through the land that lies on the other side of death, carrying us like Dante from a hell through a purgatory to a paradise. Or it may be an exploration of this world, carrying us like the Odysseus of Nikos Kazantzakis to the poles of the earth where we meet death in ice and darkness. However we tell it, our adventure appears to be somehow a story of death. Within the story of death there is a story of love like that of Odysseus and Penelope or that of Dante and Beatrice, and within the story of love and death, or containing them, there is a story of the world. We enter the story of the world in childhood, that of love in youth, and that of death in manhood.

Still, our life story, where we go from childhood to youth to manhood to age, seems to be neither a story of the world nor one of love nor one of death but something else containing all of these or contained in all of them. It may well be a simpler story like that of a child playing by the seashore. If it is, then time does not count in it so much as in the stories it contains or that contain it. The story of a child playing is simple enough to be a story of God, a story of the timeless. It can be a story of man and God like that of Jacob wrestling with God. Our life may be the story of a wrestling with the unknown, a wrestling that is like a child's playing, as easy as child's play and as hard as overcoming God.

"What kind of story are we in?" is a question we might ask if we were characters in a story and the storyteller would let us ask it. As it is, we can ask it anyway, and I would like to make it the question of this book, for stories can be told of what we do and what happens to us and what we become. It is a question about myth in the original sense of the word *mythos*, a "tale," a "story." There are stories within stories. Let us ask about them, beginning with the stories where time counts most and ending with those where it counts least, going from time to timelessness, from time to lifetime to the moment. We will come to a timelessness within time, to a time that is full of eternity. "Time," Heraclitus said, "is a child playing."[2] As we engage now in hearing and telling stories, we will be carried, I am hoping, from a time that is almost the same as death to a time that is a child playing.

# NOTES TO THE PREFACE

1. David Brewster, *Memoirs of the Life, Writings and Discoveries of Sir Isaac Newton* (Edinburgh, Constable, 1855), Vol. 2, p. 407.
2. Heraclitus, Fragment 52 in Hermann Diels and Walther Kranz, *Die Fragmente der Vorsokratiker* (Berlin, Weidmann, 1934), Vol. 1, p. 162.

ONE

# Time and the Story of Death

---

A young girl once stood barefoot on a beach in Normandy, facing the sea and singing. Yeats the poet stood behind her at a distance, listening to her song.[1] She sang of the many civilizations that had existed there and had passed away, he tells us. She sang to words of her own, but she ended each verse with the cry, "O Lord, let something remain!"

Nothing seems to remain. A man passes through the ages of life—childhood, youth, manhood, old age. Each age comes and goes, and life itself seems to go in death just as childhood does in youth and youth in manhood and manhood in age. Much the same thing seems to happen to whole civilizations. They too have their childhood, youth, manhood, and age, their birth and death, their rise and decline and fall. Nothing seems to remain after life but a death mask, a cast taken from a dead face, an impression left by a once living being. An enduring life, a life that could last through and beyond death, would have to be a deeper life than the ordinary. It would have to be some life that men have without knowing it, some current that runs far beneath the surface. To find it would be like seeing something fiery in the depths of life; it would be like hearing a rhythm in life that is not ordinarily heard. The question is whether a man, if he found such a life, could bear to live it, whether he could live at that depth, whether he could live according to that rhythm.

The deeper life would be like an undertow, like a current that flows beneath the surface, a current that sets seaward or along the beach while the waves on the surface are breaking upon the shore. The phases of life and the phases of civilization are like the waves, each phase swelling and dying away, each one rolling onto shore and breaking. A life lived on the surface is like the surf itself, like the swell of the sea that breaks upon the shore, like the foam, the splash, the sound of breaking waves. There is no swelling and breaking in the undertow, no foam, no splash, no sound. Yet it is a powerful current and may move in a direction opposite to that of the waves, may move toward the open sea while they move toward the shore. A man who gave himself to the deeper current of life might run a risk like that of a man who let himself be caught in the undertow. It might be better for him to float on the surface and let himself be carried in to shore. To live in accord with the deeper rhythm might be to ignore the surface rhythm of life. It might mean missing the normal joys and cares of childhood, youth, manhood, and age. It might mean plunging down into the depths of life to follow a light as elusive as sea fire.

The girl who stood on the shore, facing toward the sea and singing, "O Lord, let something remain!" was singing of this deeper and more enduring life. There must have been figures like her in all the civilizations of which she sang, all the civilizations that had come and gone on that shore. There must also have been figures who pointed the other way, who pointed toward the existence a man neglects when he goes in pursuit of everlasting life, toward the sacrifice, the passion, the madness, the beauty, the love that can be found in mortal existence. History is like the story of a man who meets all these figures one after another, asking each of them about life and death, asking each whether something does remain. Let us ask the question ourselves. Let us pose it to each age of history.

## 1. *The Quest of Life*

A way of asking the question might be to spend one's life searching for everlasting life. One might never attain it, but in the process of searching for it one might see many things, do many things, learn many things. The adventures that might occur on a quest of everlasting life might surpass all others simply because the quest itself surpasses all other quests, because it aims at an infinite goal. The earliest epic of adventure that is known, a tale of the first age of human history, is the story of just such a quest. It is the story of Gilgamesh and his hopeless quest of life. The original title of the epic was *He Who Knew All Things*.[2] These were the opening words of the poem, and they may well contain the moral of the story. Although Gilgamesh failed to attain everlasting life, he learned much in the process of seeking it. He searched through all space and time, traveling to faraway places, learning the history of the forgotten past. He went from person to person, from one strange figure to another, asking always about life and death.

The knowledge a man could gain on such a quest might

itself be the way to a deeper and more enduring life. This is the very sort of quest we ourselves are going on now, a journey through the ages of history, looking for insight into the mystery of life and death. We will be searching through space and time, traveling in mind to faraway places and times. We will be going from one person to another, from one historical or mythical figure to another, asking about life and death. We will undoubtedly fail like Gilgamesh to come across any way of prolonging life indefinitely, any way of preventing death. Still, we can hope like him to learn much about life and death, to acquire a knowledge of life and death. Our quest of life becomes thus a quest of knowledge. Maybe we can live, too, by the insight we gain. Maybe to live by this insight into life and death will be to live the deeper and more enduring life we seek. Maybe attaining the insight will be like seeing a light in the depths of life, hearing a rhythm beneath the familiar rhythms of life. Maybe living by it will be like following the light down into the depths, letting the rhythm become a counterpoint to the familiar rhythms. Our quest of knowledge thus becomes again a quest of life.

The story of Gilgamesh begins in the city where he is king. He is hardly conscious of his mortality in the beginning and his spirit is untempered. To temper his spirit the gods create another man who will be a match for him. When Gilgamesh meets his match, he meets for the first time another man whom he can respect. This is the first stage in the tempering of his spirit. The two become fast friends and go out on adventures together. They perform many exploits together, killing a monster who dwells in the forest and another monster who comes to plague the city. At the height of their success the goddess of the city asks Gilgamesh to make love with her and promises him immortality, but he refuses her, knowing that intercourse with the goddess is death. Then his friend takes sick and dies and everything seems to come to an end. When he sees his friend die, it is like seeing himself die. He realizes at last that he is mortal, that death awaits him. This is the second stage in the tempering of his spirit.

He sets out then on the quest of everlasting life. He has heard that there is a man who knows the secret of everlasting life, a man who has survived the great flood and who lives in the place where the sun rises. He sets out eastward to find this man and to learn from him, if he can, the secret. He comes after much travel to the mountain over which the sun rises. He finds it guarded by scorpion men. When they learn his object they try to dissuade him from going on, telling him that no mortal could ever attain everlasting life. But Gilgamesh continues on, climbing toward the sunrise. He goes on in utter darkness until he meets the sun rising. The sun too tries to dissuade him, but he begs the sun to let him live, to let him see the light of day. Then he comes down the mountain to the sea and by the sea he finds an alehouse. The alewife tries to dissuade him, telling him to enjoy life while he can and not to waste what life he has searching for everlasting life. He goes farther along the shore and finds a boatman. The boatman too tries to dissuade him but agrees at length to ferry him across to the other side. To reach the other side they must cross the Waters of Death. Finally they do reach the other shore and Gilgamesh meets there the man who has survived the flood, the man who possesses the secret of everlasting life. He tells Gilgamesh that everlasting life is a gift of the gods, not something a man can achieve for himself. So in the end Gilgamesh has to come home without ever-lasting life, with nothing to show for his quest but the wisdom he has gained. This is the final stage in the tempering of his spirit. He knows that he is mortal now and that there is no way of escaping death.

The knowledge he acquires from the quest of life is a consciousness of mortality, a tempering of the spirit. His story is really the story of how a human spirit is tempered by its encounter with death. Perhaps that is what we should expect too, from our own quest of life and knowledge, an encounter with death, a tempering of the spirit. Say we begin our quest with the idea that "Death is not an event of life," as Wittgenstein says, that "Death is not lived through."[3] Say we assume that death, when it comes, is not an event among other events, that it is rather the cessation, the absence of events. According to this notion, there is no reason why life could not be indefinitely extended. If death were an event of life like birth, then one could not live without dying, just as one cannot live without being born. If death is not an event of life, however, if life and death are like existence and non-existence, if death is no part of life, just as non-existence is no part of existence, then there may be some way of preventing death from ever occurring. This, let us say, is the idea with which we begin our quest. Perhaps it is the idea with which Gilgamesh began, the necessary assumption of any straightforward quest of unending life.

Say we end, though, with the opposite idea. Say we come in the course of our journey to learn that death is an event of life after all, that it is as much a part of life as childhood and youth and manhood and age, that there is no living without dying. If this is true, then there is no way of prolonging life indefinitely, no way of preventing death. The quest has failed, at least the straightforward quest of life without end. There is still some hope, nevertheless, of everlasting life. For if death is an event of life, then death is lived through. The two statements of Wittgenstein go together, "Death is not an event of life" and "Death is not lived through." So do the two opposite statements, "Death is an event of life" and "Death is lived through." To say that death is an event of life is to say that it is a turning point like birth or puberty or menopause, that it is, even more than menopause, a "change of life." It implies that one who dies lives through and beyond death, that death is the end of one phase and the beginning of another phase of existence. That is why Wittgenstein did not want to say it. He thought that it was a fallacy inherent in a careless way of speaking about death. If death really is an event of life, something a person undergoes just as he undergoes birth, then death is lived through. And if death is lived through, then there can be an everlasting life, not a life in which death does not occur but a life that can endure death and survive it.

Is death an event of life? Is death lived through? What life in man could endure death and survive it? The last question is the crucial one, the key to the other two. Everything depends on what life a man has in him before he dies. A woman's change of life is an image of death. If her life before the change contains little that is creative other than her fertility, then after the change she may seem only a ghost of the woman she was. If, on the contrary, there is some other creativity in her life, then her life after the change may still seem full and substantial. Something similar may happen at death. The change of life is the end of the fertility cycle; death is the end of all cycles. If nothing is going on in a man or a woman's life except the cycles of activity that death brings to an end, then after death there may be nothing left but a ghost of the former man or woman. If, on the contrary, something else is going on, something that would not have to come to a close with the cycles, then after death there may be some full and substantial existence.

The knowledge of life and death in the story of Gilgamesh is a knowledge of the cycles. It is like the wisdom of Koheleth, "There is a season for everything and a time for every purpose under heaven."[4] The things that are named by Koheleth are all seasonal activities of man: being born and dying, planting and uprooting, killing and healing, tearing down and building up, weeping and laughing, mourning and dancing, scattering and gathering, embracing and holding apart, seeking and giving up, keeping and casting away, rending and sewing, keeping silence and speaking, loving and hating, making war and making peace. Each of them has its time. If there is a life in man that can survive death, it is none of these. "Do we build a house for all time?" Gilgamesh is asked at the end of his quest. "Do we seal contracts for all time? Do brothers divide shares for all time? Does hatred persist forever in the land?"[5]

The wisdom that knows all this, that knows that all things must pass, is a tempering of the human spirit. To temper, however, can mean to soften or it can mean to harden. It can mean to soften cast iron or hardened steel by reheating it at a lower temperature; it can mean to harden steel by heating it and cooling it in oil. The knowledge that all things must pass can soften or harden the human spirit. It can soften it, taking away its arrogance and its ignorance of human mortality; it can harden it, taking away its hope. If there is a life that can survive death, it is the life of this spirit, this spirit that can live in ignorance of death and can be softened or hardened by the knowledge of death. If there is something eternal in man, it is this spirit. The stages of its life are the stages of its tempering. First there is the stage in which the spirit is untempered. Then comes the tempering, the encounter with death. That is like the steel being heated in the fire; it leads to the quest of everlasting life. Then comes the other part of the tempering, the failure of the quest. That is like the steel being cooled in oil; it can lead to the loss of all hope.

Whether the spirit is tempered or untempered, though, and whether it is softened or hardened by its tempering, it may well be able to endure death and survive it. The things that come to an end in death are all the things that have their proper times and seasons in life. Spirit is not one of these things but is rather a man's relationship to each and all of them. Its tempered or untempered quality is the quality of the relationship he has to the things of his life. Whatever the season of life in which he lives, whether it be the spring, the summer, the autumn, the winter of his life, he will have some relationship to it, awareness or unawareness, willingness or unwillingness, hope or despair. His spirit may remain untempered throughout his life, or once tempered, it may retain the same temper through one season after another, or its temper may change. The knowledge of life and death to which Gilgamesh came was a knowledge of the seasons of life and of the seasonal activities that make up a life. It tempered his spirit, hardening it and taking away all hope of everlasting life. The *story* of Gilgamesh, on the other hand, contains a higher wisdom, a knowledge of the spirit itself. It is not merely the story of the seasons in a man's life; it is the story of the tempering of a man's spirit. While Gilgamesh himself ends without hope, therefore, his story contains a hint of the eternal in man. A man's very despair in the face of death is a sign of spirit, a sign that he does not merely die but has a relationship to his own death. So too his hope and his quest of life are signs that he does not merely live but has a relationship to his own life.

The story of a man's life, according to the knowledge to which Gilgamesh comes, should be a story of seasons. It is quickly told. There is a spring, a summer, an autumn, a winter. There is childhood, youth, manhood, age. Of one ancient king in Mesopotamia it is said simply that he "went into the sea and came forth toward the mountains,"[6] he set with the sun, that is, in the western sea, and he rose with the sun in the eastern mountains. The lives of the pharaohs in Egypt were like this.[7] They rose and set with the sun. If they were thought to live on after death, it was because the cycle continued, because their lives consisted of deeds to be done ever and again, because the setting sun always rose once more. The man who survived the flood, according to the story of Gilgamesh, was like this. He was the last man of the old world, the world swallowed up in the flood, and the first man of the new world, the world that emerged from the watery chaos of the old. His story is thus the story of a repeating cycle. The ordinary man's story is that of a cycle ending in death, and so after death there is nothing left of him but a ghost. Gilgamesh at one point in his story encounters the ghost of his dead friend and learns from him that there are only ghosts in the land of the dead.[8]

The story of Gilgamesh himself, however, is a different

kind of story. It is not merely a story of seasons, of spring, summer, autumn, and winter, of childhood, youth, manhood, and age. It is a story of a man's encounter with death, of his quest of life and his attainment of wisdom. The knowledge of life and death is a knowledge of seasons. It is a man's knowledge of himself comparable with his knowledge of his crops and his herds. When the knowledge itself is included in the story, however, the story changes. It is no longer possible to say simply he "went into the sea and came forth toward the mountains." It is necessary now to say that at first he knew little of death, then he met another man who became his friend, then his friend died and he realized that he too must die, then he went in search of everlasting life but learned that it was not given to him, and then he came home again with his wisdom, his knowledge of mortality. There is a rhythm in this story that seems different from that of the seasons of life. There is a light in it too that seems brighter and deeper than the knowledge of life and death.

## 2. *The Return Home*

The first age of history was marked by man's encounter with death. It was the age when the Pyramids were built in Egypt, the age when Gilgamesh in Mesopotamia set out on the quest of everlasting life. No doubt death had been something familiar to man all through the long ages of prehistory, but in the first age of recorded history he began to strive against it, he began to strive for immortality. The failure of this striving led him to a much deeper awareness of his mortality; it tempered his spirit. The second age of history is marked by this tempered spirit and its deeds. The difference can be seen by comparing the story of Odysseus, a tale of the second age, with the story of Gilgamesh.[9] The epic of Odysseus, like that of Gilgamesh, is the tale of a quest, a journey. Odysseus travels as far as Gilgamesh, and he meets as many wonders on his way, but he does not seek everlasting life. He seeks only to reach home. It is as though the quest of everlasting life were now a thing of the past, as though man hoped now only to come home and live a mortal existence.

To reach home and to live a simple human existence can be achievements, according to this. That is something we would not have expected, starting out on our own quest of a deeper and more enduring life. One would think that living a mortal existence is the least a man can do. If it is an achievement, it will be because a man has gotten away from it somehow and has to find his way back to it again. It is not easy to come back to it, the story of Odysseus seems to say; there is much to see and do and learn on the way back; and when one finally does get back, one finds that it is not the same as before. That seems to be our situation. We have set out in search of a deeper and more enduring life, and in doing this we have turned away from mortal existence. Now our encounter with death turns us around toward mortal existence again; we have to learn how it is lived; we have a journey to go to reach it. A man who has encountered death may have to learn to live again. He is like a man who has had a stroke, who has to learn again to walk and talk.

The encounter with death occurs for Odysseus in the war against Troy. The story of the war, as it is told in the *Iliad,* is the story of Achilles and the tempering of his spirit by the death of his friend Patroclus and then the death of his enemy Hector. The first tempering is a hardening; the death of his

friend drives him to despair and cruelty. The second tempering is a softening; the death of his enemy leads him eventually to peace and compassion. The story of Odysseus, on the
other hand, as it is told in the *Odyssey,* takes place after the
war, on the return home, and is the story of a man whose
spirit has already been tempered. On the voyage home he
cannot prevent the death of his friends and companions, but
his spirit has already been hardened by the death of his com-
rades in the war. When he reaches home he brings about the
death of his enemies there, but his spirit has already been softened by the death of his enemies in the war. His sufferings
and deeds on his long journey home are the sufferings and
deeds of a tempered spirit. "Endure my heart," he says to
himself at one point. "Worse than this you have endured."[10]
His journey is the journey of a man who knows death and
who seeks to win his way back through death to life.

The journey begins in wonderland. It is a wonderland of
death, where death is not only a danger but a lure. He meets
lotus-eaters, a cyclops, a master of winds, cannibals, a witch,
ghosts, sirens, sea monsters, a goddess. At one point he comes
to the land of the dead. There he meets the ghost of Achilles
who tells him that he would rather be a slave among the living than a king among the dead. At another he is ship-
wrecked on an island inhabited by a goddess. She offers him
immortality if he will stay. At every point the question is
whether he will succumb to the fascination of death or
whether he will make his way back to the land of the living.
Finally he comes on a raft to the island of a seafaring people.
They receive him well and bring him safely home at last on
one of their ships. Now he has reached the land of the living;
he has overcome the fascination of death. The question now

is whether he will be able to win life. It is not everlasting life that he must win but only a finite human life—his wife, his home, the life he once possessed. At first he goes about his homeland in disguise; he finds his home invaded by men who are living off his substance and making proposals of marriage to his wife. Then he reveals his identity; he kills the suitors; he wins back his wife and his home and comes into his own. Now he has won through to life, a human and earthly life.

To overcome the fascination of death and to win back one's life—this seems to be the moral of his story. Death is at once dreadful and fascinating, it seems; it repels a man and yet attracts him. The dreadful side is the thing that tempers his spirit when he comes up against death. It is the dread of death that can harden him, driving him to despair, or that can soften him, teaching him compassion. The fascinating side can lure him, leading him into a wonderland where he becomes lost and unable to find his way back to life again. The wonderland is a world of fantasy. To enter it is to become a kind of lotus-eater, a man who subsists on the lotus and lives in the dreamy indolence it brings, who lives really in a dream. In the dream he encounters fascinating figures, witches, sirens, goddesses, figures who lure him further and further into wonderland. He also encounters dreadful figures, cyclops, ghosts, monsters, the figures of a nightmare. The dread aspect of death appears in the midst of the fascinating. The wonderland is a world of death, though, because as this imaginary life becomes richer and richer a man's real life, the life consisting in his relationships to other human beings, becomes poorer and poorer. It is as if he were actually dying.

There is a spiral movement here away from life. Flaubert was planning in his last years to write a story called "The Spiral."[11] It was to be about a man whose dreams became richer and richer as his life became poorer and poorer. The man was to marry the princess of his dreams just when he failed to win the woman he loved in real life. That, it seems, is the fate of the man who becomes fascinated with death and lost in the wonderland of fantasy. To break with the fascination, one can see, would be to come back to life again, to come back to the human relationships of one's real life. Still it may not be good or even possible to make the break by simply rejecting the world of fantasy. It may be necessary to face the dreadful and fascinating figures of dream and nightmare without succumbing to their dread and their fascination.

Say a man has been living on the spiral of which Flaubert spoke, say he dreams or daydreams of love, of action, but say these things are lacking in his life, say his life is loveless, actionless. Now suppose he realizes this and sets out to reverse the spiral, to travel back on the spiral path toward the center of his life. Suppose, moreover, that he has already encountered death, that his spirit has already been tempered somehow by the thought of death. The dread and fascination that death exercises over him, he may see, is what has set him spiraling away from life. Death, Heidegger says, is a "strange and unhomely thing that banishes us once and for all from everything in which we are at home."[12] According to Heidegger, there can be no homecoming for the man who has encountered death; he is banished once and for all; he can never make his way back to simple human existence and simple human relationships. According to the story of Odysseus, on the contrary, he can come home again, he can return to his life, though he has a long and dangerous journey to travel. He can come home, he can return, if he succeeds in conquering the dread and fascination of death, if he does not let himself be either daunted or lured by death.

When a man is under the spell of death he becomes fey. He becomes an outcast of life, a man who seems doomed, fated to die, and at the same time a visionary, able to see into the future, a man of foreboding, looking forward to death and calamity, a man with an otherworldly air, an otherworldly charm. To break the spell of death he must embrace a finite existence. It is the dread of death that prevents him from acting, from taking the risks involved in action. It is the fascination with death that prevents him from loving, from giving himself fully to life. To act, to love, he must somehow overcome the dread, the fascination. In breaking the spell, nevertheless, he could lose everything that he has gained from death. In ceasing to be an outcast of life, a doomed and fated man, he could become a tame man, a domesticated man. In overcoming his dread of death he could lose his vision, his foreboding, his ability to see into the future where death awaits. In overcoming his fascination with death he could lose the air, the charm of the otherworld. There ought to be some way of embracing human life and human relations, of entering into action and love, without losing his otherworldliness, his vision, his wildness. There ought to be some way of living that can go with being wild, some way of acting that can go with having vision, some way of loving that can go with a sense of the otherworld.

The human thing is not merely to live, to act, to love. It is to have a relationship to one's life, one's action, one's love, even if the relationship is simply one of consent, simply a

"Yes." There is a quality about everything human that is like that of an overtone. Every human thing—childhood, youth, manhood, and age, life, action, and love—is like a complex musical tone comprising a fundamental tone, the thing itself, and an overtone, one's relationship to the thing. Childhood is a thing of life, but a child will have a relationship to his own childhood. So it is with the youth and his youth, the man and his manhood, the old man and his old age, the living being and his life, the agent and his action, the lover and his love. A man's encounter with death, his dread of death, his fascination with death, his conquest of his dread and fascination, all have to do with these relationships, these overtones. When a man returns to his life and his human relations from an encounter with death, the overtones are likely to be changed. The fundamental tones may be the same tones that comprised his life before, but the overtones are likely to be different.

The life story is like a melody consisting of tones and overtones. Telling the story is like playing or singing the melody. It is possible to play the melody without overtones, to tell the story simply of the things of a man's life without speaking of his relationship to them. The tones then become pure tones like those of a pitch pipe or a tuning fork. It is possible, on the other hand, to sing the melody with all the overtones of the human voice, to tell the story in all its human complexity so that it becomes the story not only of the things that enter a man's life but also of his relationship to them. The tones then become the rich tones of the human voice. The story of a man like Achilles, whose spirit is tempered by his encounter with death, when the overtones, the complicating relationships, are omitted, becomes a simple story of deeds. So also

does the story of a man like Odysseus who returns to his
life from an encounter with death. The deeds of Achilles, the
deeds of Odysseus, these are the fundamental tones that constitute the melody, the things of life that constitute the story.
The tempering of the spirit by the encounter with death, the
conquering of the dread and the fascination of death in returning to life, these are the overtones that give the melody
its richness, the relationships that make the story an adventure of the human spirit.

The things of life, the fundamental tones, are things such
as being born and dying, planting and uprooting, killing
and healing, tearing down and building up, weeping and
laughing, mourning and dancing, scattering and gathering,
embracing and holding apart, seeking and giving up, keeping and casting away, rending and sewing, keeping silence
and speaking, loving and hating, making war and making
peace. Considered by themselves, apart from a man's relationship to them, they are commonplace. There is nothing
remarkable, nothing memorable about them. It is only when
the overtones are sounded, only when a man's relationship to
the things of his life is considered, that his deeds begin to
seem worthy of being remembered, worthy of living on in
memory, worthy of becoming immortal in story. Say a man
has been unconscious of his mortality and then encounters
death, the death, for example, of a friend. Say he becomes
aware not only that death is one of the things of his life but
that all the things of his life must pass. The things of his life,
if we list them, are the same as they were before, but their
quality is different, his relationship to them is different. He
may have a story now that is worth telling, a story like that
of Gilgamesh or that of Achilles. Say he is frightened away
from the things of his life by the dread of death, drawn away

from them by the fascination of death. If he comes back to them, he comes back to the same things, the same commonplace and unremarkable things, but his coming back is itself something remarkable and memorable. Here too he may have a story worth telling, a story like that of Odysseus.

There is more at issue in these negotiations with death, though, than memory and story. What is important for memory and story is that a man's deeds be worth remembering, worth telling. They could conceivably be remembered even if they weren't worth remembering or told even if they weren't worth a story. It is not the remembering and the telling themselves that count but the worth. What makes a man's life worthy of being preserved in memory and story, worthy of being kept alive after his death, is that there is a transcending of death in his life. When he becomes conscious of his mortality, when his spirit is tempered, there is a transcending in that he does not merely live and die but has a relationship to his life and death. When he overcomes the dread and fascination of death, when he returns to life from the encounter with death, the transcendence is clearer and sharper, for in a way he conquers death, he breaks the spell of death over his life. Yet he still has to die. Immortality never becomes one of the things of life, it seems. It is always an immortality of spirit, an immortality of the deeper life consisting of a man's relationships to the things of his life. It is never revealed in the tones of the song but always in the overtones.

## 3. *The Journey Through the Otherworld*

The sound of a person's voice is different in timbre and resonance for his own ear than it is for the ear of another.

Similarly the story of a person's life is different in form and quality for his own memory than it is for the memory of others. For them it is biography, for him it is autobiography; for them it is a story of deeds, for him it is a story of experience. It was characteristic of the first and second ages of history to have told the life story as a story of deeds. It becomes characteristic of a third age to tell it rather as a story of experience. The third age is, in fact, the age of the first autobiographies, for example of Augustine's *Confessions*.[13] The spirit and its immortality, latent in the story of deeds, becomes an issue now in the story of experience. Vergil's *Aeneid* written at the beginning of the third age and Dante's *Divine Comedy* written at the end have in common the conviction that the human spirit is immortal.[14] Aeneas visits the netherworld like Odysseus but instead of finding ghosts he finds immortal spirits. Dante's whole adventure takes place in the otherworld; he meets the immortal spirits of hell and purgatory and heaven. What is more, he is the central figure of his own story. Although it is an epic, his tale is like an autobiography, a story of his own experience. It begins "in the middle of the course of our life," in the midst of life on earth, but then it goes down into hell, rises up through purgatory, and ends in heaven.

A journey through the otherworld, through hell and purgatory and heaven, could be no more than a flight of fancy if there were no life in man capable of surviving death. No doubt one way of reading Dante would be to take his journey simply as an exercise of imagination, a brilliant display of invention. If there is a life of the spirit, however, a life consisting of the ins and outs of a man's relationship to the things of his life, and if this life has some serious possibility of surviving death, then his journey can be seen as a journey of the spirit, a journey during life into the realm that lies beyond death. "Hell, purgatory, and heaven," Luther says, "appear to differ as despair, near-despair, and security."[15] A man experiences hell already during life, according to Luther, when he experiences despair, purgatory when he experiences uncertainty, heaven when he experiences assurance. There seem to have been correspondences like these for Dante too, experiences in this life that anticipate the other life. If there are such experiences, then we can follow him into the otherworld by calling them to mind. We can go with him through hell and purgatory and heaven by evoking them.

"In the middle of the course of our life," he begins, "I found myself in a dark wood." Trying to find a path, he encounters a leopard, a lion, and a wolf. Then he meets the immortal spirit of Vergil who offers to guide him out of these perils. The path by which Vergil proposes to take him, though, leads down into hell itself and on beyond to purgatory and the earthly paradise. Dante follows with some hesitation. They enter the gateway to hell. The inscription on the gate reads "Abandon all hope you who enter."[16] They enter nonetheless and they encounter immediately a crowd of spirits who "have no hope of death."[17] The despair that Dante finds in hell is the despair of a spirit that is unable to die. Our own ability to follow him down there depends, it seems, on this experience, wanting to die and not being able to. He descends gradually into the circles of the incontinent, the violent, the fraudulent. There is a gamut of experience here descending from incontinence to violence to fraud. Yet the essential experience is always the suffering of the human spirit that is unable to die, the torment of the incontinent, the violent, the fraudulent spirit that wants to die and is unable to, the agony of the spirit that "cries for the second death," that cries, "Come, Death, come!"[18]

Our own starting point, the beginning of our own descent into hell, can be the experience of boredom. It is a common experience. When it goes deep, when it becomes a weariness with life, it is something like wanting to die and being unable to. It is a weariness with life and at the same time a craving for excitement. It is the despair of the incontinent spirit. Incontinence, we could say, is a flight from the weariness, a following out of the craving. As a weariness with life, boredom is a desire to die; as a craving for excitement, it is a desire to live. The two desires can coexist; the same person can desire at once to live and to die. The weariness with life leads on toward suicide, the despair of the violent spirit, and the wish never to have been born, a still more inclusive despair. "The torment of despair is precisely this," Kierkegaard says, "not to be able to die."[19] One is able to die in that death is one of the things of life; one is unable to die in that one cannot help relating to the things of one's life. The sense of being unable to die is a sense of the immortality of the spirit. Death itself, one senses, cannot relieve one of the burden of having to relate to one's life and death, of having to relate to all things of one's life in spite of one's weariness with those things and one's craving for other things.

A purgatory, a purification of the human spirit, would have to be a freeing of the spirit from this weariness and this craving. Dante's purgatory is a mountain to be climbed by the spirit, a seven-story mountain on which the spirit, as it climbs, is purified of the seven deadly sins—pride, envy, anger, sloth, covetousness, gluttony, and lust. Climbing an ordinary mountain is exhausting. The thing that strikes one most about mountain climbing when one first tries it, if one does it by walking and scrambling up, is not the danger of falling so much as the weariness of it and the endurance it requires. Climbing the mountain of purgatory, according to Dante, is almost the reverse of climbing an ordinary mountain. "This mountain," Vergil, his guide, tells him, "is such that at the beginning down below it is always wearisome, and as a man goes up higher it becomes less tiring."[20] As he climbs, a man is purified of weariness and craving. The higher he goes, the easier it becomes, until, when he feels no more weariness and craving at all, he is at the top.

The desolation one feels when one is bored, when one is weary with the things of one's life and craves other things, is hell and purgatory both. It is hell when one is in despair. It is purgatory when there is hope. When a man is doing something that is exhausting, when he is climbing or running, for instance, he becomes much more weary if he loses hope, if he despairs. There is a weariness that is in the heart, a heaviness of heart that somehow increases the weariness and heaviness that is in the arms and legs. When a man loses hope of reaching the goal to which he is climbing or running, or when he loses hope of reaching it in time, he becomes much more weary than he should be for the effort he has made. When he begins to hope, on the contrary, when he begins to believe that he will reach it, that he will be in time, then the weariness and the heaviness can seem to drop away and he may begin to feel instead an ease and a lightness.

What hope can there be, though, when one is weary of the things of one's life and craves other things? How can one escape the things of one's life? How can one help relating to them? There is no hope of escaping the things of one's life, it is true, of escaping the necessity of relating to them, of escaping the life of the spirit. There is hope, nevertheless, of escaping the weariness and the craving themselves. There is hope of a new relationship to the things of one's life. Heaven would have to be this, a new life, a new relationship in which the old weariness and craving have disappeared. Dante's descent into hell is a journey to the center of the earth. The bottommost point of hell is the earth's center of gravity. The crucial moment, the turning point, comes when he passes the center of gravity and begins to climb up on the other side of the earth. As he climbs out and continues climbing on up the mountain of purgatory, as he gets farther and farther from the center of gravity, he becomes lighter and lighter. When he finally reaches the summit of purgatory, he is light enough to rise into the sky, into the regions of heaven. All the heaviness and the drag of weariness and craving are gone. Up till now Vergil has been his guide. From now on his guide is Beatrice, a woman he describes in his autobiography, *The New Life*, the woman who becomes the turning point of his life dividing it into "old" and "new," the woman who led him into his "new life."

The heaviness, the drag of the spirit comes, it seems, from an unwillingness, from a No. It is a No to the things of one's life, but ultimately it is a No to the life of the spirit itself. One is unwilling to live the life of the spirit, unwilling to be in the position of having to relate to the things of one's life, of being responsible for them, of having to reflect on them, of having to take an attitude toward them. "Why can't I simply live and die?" one asks. This basic unwillingness leads then to boredom, to weariness with the things of one's life and craving for other things. One is tired of having to relate to the same old things. One is tired above all of having to relate. A new thing—for example, a new person—if it—or he—were to enter one's life, would bring only a passing impression of relief if the unwillingness were to remain unchanged. The new thing would merely take its place among the old things. There would be no new life unless the new thing or the new person were to inspire one to live the life of the spirit, to say Yes, to become willing. That is what Beatrice seems to have done for Dante. She inspired him to live a higher, a deeper life, to live the life of the spirit.

It is better, according to Kierkegaard, to be inspired by a woman than to live with her.[21] Whether it is really better or not, that is what happened to Dante. He was inspired by Beatrice but he never lived with her. His *New Life* and his *Divine Comedy* end with him being inspired by her. The *Odyssey* ends, by contrast, with Odysseus coming home to live with Penelope. Both the journey of Dante and that of Odysseus end with a Yes, but the Yes of Odysseus is to the things of his life while the Yes of Dante is to the life of the spirit. There is no disagreement between them if one conceives the life of the spirit, as we have been conceiving it, to be the relationship one has to the things of one's life. Yes to the relationship is Yes to the things. Yes to the relationship, nevertheless, goes much further. When Dante reaches the bottom of hell he says, "I did not die and I did not remain alive."[22] When he reaches the height of heaven, he says he is moved by "the love that moves the sun and the other stars."[23] The compass of the spirit is thus very great. The nadir is a point where a man seems neither dead nor alive, the zenith a point where he lives supremely, moved by the love pervading the universe. A Yes to the life of the spirit is a Yes to the whole range of experience, from the bottom of hell to the height of heaven.

There is a gamut of experience comprising simply the things of life, being born and dying, planting and uprooting, killing and healing, tearing down and building up, weeping and laughing, mourning and dancing, scattering and gathering, embracing and holding apart, seeking and giving up, keeping and casting away, rending and sewing, keeping silence and speaking, loving and hating, making war and making peace. A man could run this gamut, one can see, without ever reaching the bottom of hell or the height of heaven. It is like the circle of horizontal directions, north and south, east and west, northeast and southwest, northwest and southeast. Each direction is coupled with its opposite. One can make the full circle, can face successively in all directions, by turning around on the same spot. The nadir and the zenith do not lie on the circle, but below it and above it. They are opposite points on the sphere that encloses the circle. So it is to be neither dead nor alive, to be moved by the love that moves the sun and the stars. These are experiences that do not occur on the simple gamut of experience. They lie below it and above it. They belong to a greater gamut, the life of the spirit, which encompasses the simple gamut as a sphere does a circle.

An azimuth, a position on the horizon, always goes with a nadir and a zenith, an uttermost point below the observer and an uttermost point overhead. There is likewise for each thing on the gamut of ordinary experience a nadir and a zenith of the spirit. Say one is laughing and dancing. There is an entire range of situations one can be in, from a laughing and dancing in which one is neither dead nor alive, when one laughs and dances because nothing matters, to a laughing and dancing in which one is moved by the love that moves the sun and the stars, when one laughs and dances because everything matters. In between there are the more usual situations, when one laughs and dances because something does not matter or because something does matter. The nadir of the spirit is a purely negative relationship to the things of life; nothing matters. One is not alive, for none of the things of life matter, and yet one is not dead, for the relationship, however negative, is still a relationship. The zenith of the spirit is a purely affirmative relationship; everything matters. One is moved by the love that moves the sun and the stars, in that one cares, as that love cares, for all the things of life.

It is easier to run the gamut of ordinary experience than it is to go from the nadir to the zenith of the spirit. It is easier to go from laughing to crying than it is to go from laughing because nothing matters to laughing because everything matters. Still, there is a correspondence between the nadir and the zenith, between one extreme and the other, which enables a man who experiences the one to imagine the other. One can live always in between, but to reach the zenith it seems necessary to consent to the whole compass of the spirit and somehow make the great journey from one extreme to the other. Although it is not merely an exercise of imagination, the journey requires imagination. It is, as Dante called it, "high fantasy," *alta fantasia.*[24] One could not even imagine what it would be for everything to matter if one could not imagine also what it would be for nothing to matter. To actually make the journey, to begin in the middle where some things matter and some things do not matter and then to go down to the nadir where nothing matters and then up to the zenith where everything matters leaves one at the zenith. Can a man live at the point where everything matters? Can he go through life moved by the love that moves the sun and the stars?

## 4. *The Exploration of This World*

If one tries to live at the zenith, one may find oneself slipping back and forth between the zenith and the nadir. One may find oneself exploring, in fact, the entire sphere of experience, from pole to pole and from meridian to meridian. The third age of history, Dante's age, sought to reach the zenith; the fourth age, our own, slips back and forth between the zenith and the nadir and seeks rather to explore the whole world of experience. Dante, when he has reached almost the nadir of his journey, encounters in hell a man who is like a prototype of our own age. It is Odysseus, a hero of the second age, but it is an Odysseus who has a sequel to add to the story told by Homer. "Neither fondness for my son, nor reverence for my old father, nor the due love that should have made Penelope happy," Odysseus tells Dante, "could conquer in me the ardor I had to become experienced in the world and in human vices and worth."[25] Odysseus could not remain at home but became an explorer and met his death trying to explore the other side of the earth. Nikos Kazantzakis in *The Odyssey: A Modern Sequel* took up Dante's suggestion and wrote in our own age a sequel to Homer's story, an enormous epic several times as long as Homer's.[26] According to Kazantzakis' tale, Odysseus becomes an explorer of the earth and of the realm of human experience. He does what a man of

our time might desire to do, and when he has run the entire
gamut he meets his death at the South Pole.

A person living in our time, if he tries to live like a man of
the previous age, if he tries to point himself toward the zenith and be concerned only with rising to the height a human
being can reach, is likely to find himself fearing that he will
miss something in life, that he will reach only the height but
never the depth and breadth of human life. If he seeks like
Dante to be moved by the love that moves the sun and the
stars, he is likely to find himself fearing that he will miss the
experience of intimate love. If he seeks like Plotinus to rise
from the body to soul to mind to God, he is likely to find himself fearing that in seeking God he will neglect and leave behind the body, the soul, and the mind. Let these fears be our
starting point now. Imagine a man who is troubled by them.
Say he sets out now to explore the realms he has neglected.
Say he includes the old ideal of reaching the height only as
part of the more comprehensive new goal of exploring the
whole world of experience. What will happen to him?

The man Kazantzakis imagines in his *Odyssey* is merely
restless at the start. He has not yet attempted to reach the zenith of human life. His restlessness, though, causes him to
set out on a voyage to explore the height and the depth and
the breadth of human experience. What happens to him may
be an indication of what will happen to the man we are imagining. The voyage is at first a journey with God. Seven
faces of God appear: the first the face of an animal, the second that of a fighting man, the third that of a lover, the
fourth that of a thinker, the fifth a sorrowful face, the sixth
a serene face slightly smiling, the seventh a smooth and transparent surface.[27] Each corresponds to a stage in Odysseus'

own development as he goes from one adventure to another, sailing across the Mediterranean and then up the Nile. The last stages occur when he has withdrawn into solitude on a mountain in Africa. When he returns from solitude he and his companions build an ideal city based on his vision of God, but the city is destroyed by an earthquake. At this he rejects the notion of God, and from now on death instead of God becomes his constant companion. The journey henceforth is a journey with death and toward death.

It is at this point, when the journey ceases to be a journey with God and becomes a journey with death, that Kazantzakis' hero begins to resemble the man we are imagining. He has now attempted to reach the zenith of the spirit, to commune with God, but he turns from that to life as a whole. "My soul," he tells himself, "your voyages have been your native land."[28] There is no native land now, neither the homeland that Homer's Odysseus sought nor the heaven that Dante sought. He has forsaken his homeland, his wife, and his son, and he has given up the quest of heaven. There remains only the journey itself, his voyages. Death therefore becomes his companion and his destination. "Forward, my lads, sail on," he cries, "for Death's breeze blows in a fair wind!"[29] He meets a prince who is like Gotama the Buddha, who is horror-stricken at the sight of death, but Odysseus tells him "Death is the salt that gives life its tasty sting."[30] Then he meets a prostitute with whom he agrees that in love "There's no you or I, but Life and Death are One,"[31] but he goes on to add, "This One is empty air."[32] He travels on, meets a hermit who asks him, "Why were we born?"[33] but he tells the hermit only to put his ear to the earth and listen. He meets a figure who is like Don Quixote, admires him but has no desire to live as he does in a world of fancy. Last of all, when he has come to the southernmost tip of Africa, he meets a Negro fisher lad who is like Jesus, who speaks of love and says earth is a path to the sky, but Odysseus answers, "That man is free who strives on earth with not one hope."[34] Then finally he sets sail for the South Pole. He sees his death looking like his twin, sitting on the prow of his boat. His boat shatters on an iceberg, and he dies clinging to the iceberg and recalling all the memories of his life.

When a man turns from the zenith to the whole compass of life, Kazantzakis' story seems to say, his life ceases to be a journey with God and to God and becomes instead a journey with death and to death. When he no longer seeks the height alone but seeks the height and the depth and the breadth of human life, his journey ceases to have any goal other than itself. It becomes a journey for the sake of the journey, for the sake of the experience. So when the journey is over, when the experience is complete, there is no more. The journey ends in death. Hegel's *Phenomenology of Mind* is probably the classical description of the journey for the sake of the experience. It is a travelogue of the human spirit. Its original title was *Science of the Experience of Consciousness.*[35] It suggests that the upshot of man's journey through life is the experience of consciousness, the conscious experience of the height and depth and breadth of life and ultimately the conscious experience of consciousness itself. So when the experience of consciousness is consummated, one might infer, the journey is over and there is nothing more. Hegel remarked, however, that for him personally the journey he describes was a "voyage of discovery."[36] The experi-

ence of consciousness was not so much the goal as the upshot. The goal was discovery.

The "experience of consciousness" is a description one
might give to one's life thus far, to the journey one has already made. One's life thus far has become experience and
exists in one's memory. The description is rather unsuitable,
though, for the remainder of one's life, for the journey one
has still to make. The journey yet to be made would better
be called a "voyage of discovery." The goal of a voyage of
discovery is somewhat indeterminate, for one does not know
in advance what one is going to discover. After a voyage has
been completed one can compose a travelogue in which all
the incidents of the voyage are narrated in such a way as
to lead up to discoveries one has made. But before the voyage
has been undertaken one cannot do this because one doesn't
know what the discoveries will be. Both the "experience of
consciousness" and the "voyage of discovery" can be ways of
life. I can devote my life to gaining the experience of consciousness. I can make my life a voyage of discovery.

If I devote my life to gaining the experience of consciousness, to bringing everything in me to consciousness, to giving
everything a conscious form, then at the end of my life, when
death comes, I can hope that there will be nothing left
for death to take, that I will have exhausted the possibilities
of life. "The archer has fooled you, Death," Kazantzakis says
of his Odysseus at the end, "he's squandered all your
goods."[37] Making this my aim, however, I make my life a
journey with death and to death. When one seeks to experience everything, when one does what one does for the sake of
experience, one is seeking to reduce one's life to experience,
to what it will be in memory, to what it will be when it is

past. Death thus becomes one's goal and one's constant companion. One's goal is experience, the experience of consciousness, and yet one's goal is death. Experience, we could say,
is life lived, life already lived. When I make it my goal to
have lived, to be able to say at the end "I have lived," then I
live in hope of having lived and in fear of not having lived,
in hope of a complete life and in fear of an incomplete life. I
live with death before me and behind me. Death before me is
the death I hope for, that of a life already lived; death behind
me is the death I fear, that of a life not yet lived.

If I make my life a voyage of discovery, on the other hand,
I do not hope to meet a certain kind of death ahead of me or
fear to be surprised by another kind of death behind me. I
expect rather to meet the unknown; I live with the unknown
before me and behind me; the unknown becomes my goal
and my companion on the way. If my life has been previously
a journey with God and to God, it does not cease to be that
when I make it a voyage of discovery. It becomes rather a
journey with an unknown God and to an unknown God, a
God whom I come to know as I make the discoveries on my
voyage. The question for me is not "Is there a God?" so much
as "What is God?" The question "Is there a God?" supposes
that one already understands what God would be if there
were a God. It supposes that no voyage of discovery is necessary. The question "What is God?" on the contrary, calls for
a voyage of discovery, for a whole lifetime of discovery. As
I explore the height and the depth and the breadth of life,
each discovery I make about life is a discovery about God,
each is a step with God, a step toward God.

As I go on from discovery to discovery, it is true, my voyage becomes an experience. It becomes, in fact, an experience

of consciousness. I become conscious of the things of my life
and conscious of my consciousness of them. I become a conscious self. If I keep a log of my voyage, if I keep a diary or
write an autobiography, it will be a story of experience, a
story of the experience of consciousness, a story of self-realization. The only danger is that I or someone else reading the
story will be led to believe that the experience of consciousness or the conscious self is the goal of life. If the conscious
self becomes my goal, I become engaged in an effort to attain
full consciousness, to leave nothing to the dark of unconsciousness, to reach a place where there is no darkness. The
voyage then becomes a polar voyage, a journey to the land of
the midnight sun where the sun remains always above the
horizon in the summer. Heinrich Heine called Hegel "the
man who sailed around the world of the spirit and intrepidly
advanced to the North Pole of thought where one's brain
freezes in the abstract ice."[38]

Actually the brain freezes only when discovery ceases to
occur, and discovery ceases when one believes that one has
reached full consciousness and there is nothing more to discover. The polar summer when the sun never sets is followed
by the polar winter when the sun never rises. When Odysseus meets his death at the South Pole, Kazantzakis has it
that the sun sets and the polar night begins.[39] The way
through the ice, it seems, is to continue to live with the
unknown and to move into the unknown, to continue the
voyage of discovery, to realize that the conscious self is not
the consummation of life.[40] When one becomes conscious of
the things of one's life and conscious of one's consciousness
of them, it can seem that there is nowhere else to go, that
nothing remains unconscious. In reality, though, the things

of one's life continue to change as one's life goes on, and so one's consciousness of them can change too and also one's consciousness of consciousness. The conscious self, that is, proves to be no one point on the globe of life, one of the poles for example, but is simply the point anywhere on the globe where one happens to be at a given time. It is not the goal or should not be the goal; it is merely and always the point one has reached so far in the voyage of discovery.

No one relationship to the things of life, therefore, no one form of the conscious self, however conscious it may be, is enduring. If there is something that endures in man, it is the life of the spirit that carries on from one relationship to another. When the immortality of the human spirit is denied in our times, what is being denied usually is the immortality of the conscious self. What is truly immortal, however, is not the conscious self, frozen at some point in its career and preserved forever, but the life of the spirit. "The life of the spirit is not one that shuns death and keeps clear of destruction," Hegel says. "It endures death and in death maintains its being."[41] Hegel may mean that the human spirit lives in its experience of consciousness and experience is a kind of death in that it is life lived. The saying seems true, nevertheless, in a more substantial sense. The spirit lives in its adventures, in its voyage of discovery, and these adventures never cease. Death itself is one of the adventures of the spirit, a voyage with the unknown into the unknown, a voyage with the unknown God and to the unknown God.

The adventures of the spirit, recounted in the epics of different ages, seem to form a sequence. We can narrate them as though they were a single tale, as though they were the story of one and the same man. The story begins with a man's encounter with death. He sees his own death in that of a friend. He has always known that men are mortal, that he is a man, and therefore that he is mortal, but he has never had a concrete sense of his own mortality. Now he sees, he realizes that he is mortal. His first response is to search for some means of conquering death, some way to immortality. We can imagine his quest of everlasting life as a journey toward the east, toward the place where the sun rises. His journey begins in the morning with the darkness behind him in the west and the sun rising before him in the east. As he goes on, though, the sun rises on up to the zenith and then begins to go down behind him in the west. Darkness appears before him in the east; it is only the earth's shadow, but as the sun sets behind him the shadow rises quickly to the zenith. His quest fails; he finds only death and darkness ahead of him.

Now he turns back. His quest of everlasting life has taken him far away from home. He realizes that there is no way of avoiding death. So he seeks to return home and live the mortal life that is given to him. His journey now, we can imagine, is a journey toward the west. As the sun rises behind him he sees the earth's shadow again, this time in the west, but the shadow falls quickly below the horizon. He knows that death is ahead of him, but it drops in back of the life that is ahead. While he continues on, the sun rises to noon and then begins to go down in front of him. It was only the earth's shadow that was falling below the horizon in the morning, but in the evening it is the sun itself. There is something bright and fascinating about death, he sees, something radiant like the setting sun as well as something dark like the earth's shadow. He becomes fascinated with death; he finds it difficult to take his eyes off the brightness and the radiance and fix them on the twilight colors of his life. It almost seems to him that his goal is where the sun sets rather than home, death rather than life. He resists the fascination, nevertheless, and finally does reach home.

After he has been home a while and has returned to his everyday life, he begins to feel restless again. It is difficult for a man who has known the quest of everlasting life, who has known the dread and fascination of death, to be satisfied with an everyday human existence. So he sets out once more, not to search for a way of prolonging life nor to follow the lure of death—these things are behind him—but to discover what life there may be beyond death. Contemplating his journey, he looks no longer toward the horizons, toward sunrise and sunset, but toward the zenith and the nadir, toward the point where the sun stands at noon and the point where it stands at midnight. The nadir where the sun stands at midnight is the zenith on the other side of the earth. He must travel, it seems to him, from noon to midnight, from the zenith of this life to the zenith of the other life. He must journey in spirit from earth to heaven, passing through hell and purgatory. He begins the journey at the noonday of life, at the height of his powers, and he seeks to reach the height that is opposite to the one at which he stands. He seeks to move with the sun from noon to midnight, to let himself be moved by "the love that moves the sun and the other stars."

As he makes his journey, however, he realizes that in traveling from one side of the earth to the other he is exploring the earth. By going from the height where he stands at the height of his powers to the opposite height, he is running the gamut of experience. He decides to continue the journey, therefore, not only to reach the opposite point but to explore the whole earth, to explore the entire realm of human life. He decides to look for God not only at the height but also in the depth and breadth of human experience. Looking for God everywhere, at the nadir as well as the zenith, in the meridians as well as the poles of life, he discovers a dark as well as a bright side of God. The voyage to the poles leads to the discovery of the polar summer in which the midnight sun stays always above the horizon, but it leads also to the discovery of the polar winter, the polar night in which the sun no longer rises. God becomes for him an unknown God or a God who is both known and unknown, both bright and dark, and his life becomes a voyage of discovery in which each new discovery is a further discovery of God.

The girl who stood facing the sea and singing, "O Lord, let something remain!" was singing to God, to a God known and unknown. It was a known God who was addressed "O Lord." It was an unknown God, a God of unknown power and purpose, who was asked, "Let something remain." If something does remain, it is because man does not merely live and die. It is because man has a relationship to his life and death. If something does remain, it is the life of the spirit. Each of the civilizations of which the girl was singing was an adventure of the spirit, as was each of the ages of which we have been speaking, whether the adventure was a quest of everlasting life or a return home to mortality, whether it was a journey through the otherworld or an exploration of this world. Yet it was fitting that she was singing to God. Man can relate to his life and death; he can live the life of the spirit. When he lives it, though, he is setting out into the unknown. He is facing the unknown, the unknown God. He is like the girl facing the sea. As he voyages out into the unknown he discovers the life of the spirit. As he lives it he discovers it, and as he discovers it he discovers that something does remain.

# NOTES TO CHAPTER ONE

1. William Butler Yeats, *A Vision* (New York, Collier, 1966), p. 220.
2. The opening words and title, *Sa nagba imuru*, could also be translated "He Who Saw Everything," as in J. B. Pritchard, *Ancient Near Eastern Texts* (Princeton, Princeton University Press, 1955), pp. 72ff. Cf. my discussion of the Gilgamesh epic in *The City of the Gods* (New York, Macmillan, 1965), pp. 2ff.
3. Ludwig Wittgenstein, *Tractatus Logico-Philosophicus* (New York, Harcourt, Brace, 1922), 6.4311.
4. Ecclesiastes 3:1. The biblical quotations throughout the book are based on the King James version, but I have altered the sentence structure here and there.
5. Cf. Pritchard, op. cit., p. 92.
6. Ibid., p. 266.
7. Cf. my discussion of Egyptian ideas of life and death in *The City of the Gods*, pp. 16ff.
8. Cf. Pritchard, op. cit., p. 98.
9. Cf. my comparison of the two epics in *The City of the Gods*, pp. 67ff.
10. *Odyssey*, XX, 18. Cf. Homer, *The Odyssey*, tr. by A. T. Murray (London, Heinemann; New York, Putnam, 1931), Vol. 2, p. 275. I have changed the wording of the second clause.
11. Cf. Yeats, op. cit., p. 70.
12. Martin Heidegger, *An Introduction to Metaphysics*, tr. by Ralph Manheim (Garden City, N.Y., Doubleday Anchor, 1961), p. 133. I have changed the word "alien" in the translation to the more literal "unhomely" (*unheimlich*).
13. Cf. my discussion of Augustine's *Confessions* in *A Search for God in Time and Memory* (New York, Macmillan, 1970), pp. 45ff.
14. Cf. my discussion of the *Aeneid* in *The City of the Gods*, pp. 113ff., and my discussion of the *Divine Comedy*, ibid., pp. 163ff., and in *A Search for God in Time and Memory*, pp. 77ff.

15. Thesis 16 of the *Ninety-five Theses*. The translation is mine. Cf. Luther's own commentary on this thesis in Pelikan and Lehman, *Luther's Works* (Philadelphia, Fortress, 1957), Vol. 31, p. 130. Cf. my discussion and use of this idea in *A Search for God in Time and Memory*, pp. 79ff.

16. Dante, *Inferno*, III, 9. The translations are mine. The text of Dante that I am using is Paget Toynbee, ed., *Le opere di Dante Alighieri* (Oxford, Oxford University Press, 1924).

17. Ibid., 46.

18. Ibid., I, 117, and XIII, 118.

19. Sören Kierkegaard, *Sickness unto Death*, tr. by Walter Lowrie (Princeton, Princeton University Press, 1968), p. 150.

20. Dante, *Purgatorio*, IV, 88ff.

21. Cf. Kierkegaard, *Stages on Life's Way*, tr. by Walter Lowrie (New York, Schocken, 1967), p. 70.

22. Dante, *Inferno*, XXXIV, 25.

23. Dante, *Paradiso*, XXXIII, 145.

24. Ibid., 142.

25. Dante, *Inferno*, XXVI, 94ff.

26. Nikos Kazantzakis, *The Odyssey: A Modern Sequel*, tr. by Kimon Friar (New York, Simon and Schuster, 1958). Note that Kazantzakis had already translated Dante's *Divine Comedy* into modern Greek; ibid., pp. ixff.

27. Ibid., Bk. V, ll. 598ff.

28. Ibid., XVI, 959.

29. Ibid., XXIV, 1396.

30. Ibid., XVIII, 912.

31. Ibid., 1147, 1149.

32. Ibid., 1208, 1219.

33. Ibid., XIX, 495.

34. Ibid., XXI, 1351.

35. Cf. Martin Heidegger, *Hegel's Concept of Experience* (New York, Harper & Row, 1970), p. 7. The phrase occurs still in Hegel's Introduction; cf. Hegel, *Phenomenology of Mind*, tr. by J. B. Baillie (London, Allen & Unwin, 1964), p. 144.

36. The word Hegel used was *Entdeckungsreisen*, according to

Karl Rosenkranz, a pupil of Hegel's, in *Hegels Leben* (Berlin, Duncker & Humbolt, 1844), p. 204.

37. Kazantzakis, op. cit., Bk. XXIII, l. 34.
38. Heinrich Heine, as quoted by Walter Kaufmann in *Hegel: A Reinterpretation* (Garden City, N.Y., Doubleday, 1965), p. 356.
39. Or so one could interpret the epilogue to the sun in Kazantzakis, op. cit., p. 776. Cf. the prologue, ibid., pp. 1ff., also addressed to the sun.
40. Cf. my discussion of "self" and "soul" in *A Search for God in Time and Memory*, pp. 172ff., and my discussion of "being" and "consciousness" in Chap. 7 of *The Way of All the Earth* (New York, Macmillan, 1972).
41. Hegel, op. cit., p. 93. Baillie writes "mind" here instead of "spirit" as he does also in the title *Phenomenology of Mind*. The term "spirit," though, is a closer rendering of Hegel's term *Geist* and is more in accordance with the terminology I have been using in this chapter.

# TWO

# Lifetime and the Life Story

---

When a man's life has become a voyage into the unknown, a voyage with only the unknown for a companion, he may begin to long for human companionship. He may begin to long for a human life with which to match his life. "Let me look into a human eye," Ahab exclaims in *Moby Dick*. "It is better than to gaze into sea or sky, better than to gaze upon God."[1]

Living with only the unknown for a companion is like being a long time at sea, always watching the sea and sky, always gazing and yet never seeing the sea and sky return one's gaze. One longs finally to gaze into something that will gaze back, to look into a human eye. When one looks into a human eye, one sees another who sees oneself. One sees in the pupil of the other's eye a tiny image of oneself. One sees there also a reflection of the sea and the sky; one gazes still upon God. Sharing the life of another human being, even momentarily, requires a shifting of standpoints, a shifting from one's own perspective to that of the other. It is indeed like looking into the other's eye and seeing there the images of what the other sees. Remembering one's own past life can require a similar shifting of standpoints, a shifting, for instance, from the perspective of one's manhood to that of one's childhood or one's youth. It is like looking into the eye of the child or the youth that one was and seeing there a tiny image of oneself as a man, the child's or the youth's vision of the man, and seeing there also the sea and the sky that the child or the youth saw, facing the unknown that he faced.

Sharing the life of another human being is like remembering one's own life and remembering is like sharing the life of another. A man has to have within himself what he shares and remembers. The child and the youth must live on in the man if he is to go back to their standpoints. He must be able through his own childhood and youth and manhood to understand that of another if he is to go over to the standpoint of the other. Before he remembers and shares, he seems to have nothing but the standpoint where he stands, gazing out into the sea and sky, gazing upon God the unknown. After he remembers, he seems richer, he seems to have within him the youth and the child. After he shares, he even seems to have within him the other human being. When he comes back again to his own perspective, when he gazes directly again into the sea and sky, he sees with new eyes. He sees with the eyes of the child and the youth as well as with those of the man. He even sees with the eyes of the other.

What does he see? Ordinarily a man sees only what he can observe from his own perspective. He understands the things of life in terms of his own relationship to them. If he sees with the eyes of the child and the youth as well as the man, though, if he sees with the eyes of the other, he sees from perspectives other than his own. He is able to see beyond his own relationship; he gains, in fact, a new and fuller relationship to the things of life. God remains the unknown to him: God is the unknown to the child, to the youth, to the other. Yet when a man comes to know the unknown as the child does, as the youth does, as the other does, he gains a vision of God that he did not have before. Let us see what such a vision would be. Let us examine our own lives and the lives of others. Let us try remembering our own lives and examining the remembrance of other lives in autobiographies, and let us see what it would be to see with the eyes of the child, the youth, the man, and the other man.

## 1. *The Child and the Story of the World*

If we go back in memory from manhood to youth to childhood, we come eventually to a point where memory fails. It is not a precise point. We go back through consecutive recollections to scattered recollections, and it is not clear which of the scattered recollections is earliest. Sergei Aksakoff begins his autobiography of childhood with a chapter entitled "Scattered Recollections."[2] Then he goes on to "Consecutive Recollections" and then to a detailed account of the places and times and journeys of his childhood. If we go back in our own memory, we come first upon the detailed memories of later childhood, then the consecutive memories of earlier childhood, and then the scattered memories of the earliest years. The beginning of life remains hidden in darkness. Recalling childhood is like going back through light to darkness, and telling the story of it is like coming forward from darkness into light. The story begins like a story of creation. "In the beginning the world was covered with darkness. There was no sun, no day. The perpetual night had no moon or stars."³ These are the opening words of Geronimo's auto-biography. He begins the story of his life by telling the Apache story of creation. Augustine ends his *Confessions* by telling the story of creation from Genesis: "In the beginning God created heaven and earth. And the earth was without form, and void; and darkness was upon the face of the deep."⁴

There is some profound link, it seems, between the story of a man's life and the story of his world. The story of his world is his myth, the story in which he lives, the greater story that encompasses the story of his life. To discover his myth he must go deeper into his life than he would if he were going to tell only his life story. He must somehow rediscover the world he discovered in the beginning of his life, the world into which he entered as a child. He must see it again with the eyes of a child; he must see it as a new world, an unexpected world. When he was a child he learned the story of the world from others. He learned the story and he also learned how to relate to the world. The relationship he learned to the world may have told a more eloquent story about the world than the story he heard told in words. He may have heard, for example, the story from Genesis, that in the beginning God created heaven and earth. His relationship to the world, however, may tell quite another story. That other story, the one his relationship tells, is his myth.

"In what myth does man live nowadays? In the Christian myth? Do you live in it? Then do we no longer have any myth? But then what is your myth—the myth in which you do live?"⁵ These are questions that Carl Jung says he asked himself at the turning point of his life. Let us ask ourselves these same questions. There are stories of the world corresponding to each of the epic adventures—the quest of life, the return home to mortality, the journey through the otherworld, the exploration of this world. The story told in the first and second ages of history, the ages of the quest of life and the return home to mortality, is that the world man knows came about by the killing of a primeval monster. The *Enuma Elish*, a creation epic of the first age, tells of the killing of a primeval monster named Tiamat; Hesiod's *Theogony*, a creation story of the second age, tells of the killing of a monster named Typhoeus. The story told in the third age, derived from Genesis, omits mention of the monster (called Leviathan elsewhere in the Bible) and has it that the world was created from nothingness. The monster reappears, nevertheless, in the fourth age and lives unconquered in the world. The story, as it is told in Melville's *Moby Dick*, is the story of man's fruitless efforts to conquer the monster and set the world right.

Is this then the story in which we live? The story Melville tells is that of a sea captain named Ahab who has lost a leg to a great white whale named Moby Dick. The captain sets sail to seek vengeance but is killed trying to kill the whale. Moby Dick is like the monsters in the old creation myths, Tiamat and Typhoeus. The difference is that Moby Dick is still at large; the monster has not been overcome. It is as though we were living in the midst of a creation story that is still unfinished. The world we live in, if this is the kind of story we are in, is like the primeval world of the ancient myths, the infested world in which evil has not yet been conquered. What is more, there appear to be no gods to conquer the monster for us, to rid the world of evil. It appears to be up to man to struggle against evil, to sail out against it like Ahab. Yet if man sails against the monster, if he attempts to set the world right, if he tries to destroy evil, Melville's story seems to say, he will only destroy himself. He will end like Ahab, plunging the harpoon into Moby Dick and then being caught round the neck by the running line and jerked down into the sea after the diving whale.

Describing the stages of life by which one comes to a view like his, Melville speaks of going "through infancy's unconscious spell, boyhood's thoughtless faith, adolescence's doubt (the common doom), then scepticism, then disbelief, resting at last in manhood's pondering repose of If."[6] We can test this in our own memory, starting with manhood and working our way back through youth to childhood. The "If," it seems, is the experience of a man who has nothing human to stand between him and God. He is like Ahab exclaiming, "Let me look into a human eye; it is better than to gaze into sea or sky, better than to gaze upon God." When a man stands alone like this, gazing into sea and sky, gazing upon God, he feels at once too close to God and too far from him. There is nothing human to separate him from God and nothing human to join him to God. He finds God too near and too far, too near in that he feels God-ridden, obsessed with God like Melville, too far in that God appears to him nevertheless to be absent from the world, to be non-existent even, and evil appears to go unchecked in the world.

The "If" is "If there is a God." When one feels the absence of God and the unchecked power of evil in the world, it seems that there is no God. When one feels oneself obsessed with this absence and this power, on the other hand, it seems that there is no escape from God. If I feel alone like Ahab now in manhood, gazing into sea and sky, gazing upon

God, longing to look into a human eye, I may find as I recall my past life that I was alone already in youth, that perhaps I did not dare then to look into a human eye, that I dared only to gaze into sea and sky, only to gaze upon God. The beginning of youth is the age of puberty when sexuality rises in a person and confronts him with the dilemmas of love just as the beginning of manhood is the rise of mortality, the growing consciousness of mortality, when a person sees his youth passing. The fear of love may have been as great in my youth as the fear of death is in my manhood, and I may have been as alone then in the face of love as I am now in the face of death.

Going back still further to the time when neither love nor death had become a dilemma, I may find that I was alone already in childhood, especially in late childhood. A child's fear is not a fear of death or of love, it seems, so much as a more undifferentiated fear of the unknown. I may remember being alone as a child in the face of the unknown, having to change schools, for instance, and to leave a familiar for an unfamiliar world. I may remember my sorrow and despair, how I could not see beyond the unfamiliarity of the new world, how I did not realize that it would become as familiar as the old. "We should not make light of the troubles of children," Yeats says in his *Reveries over Childhood and Youth*. "They are worse than ours, because we can see the end of our trouble and they can never see any end."[7] Not having any long-range pursuits to carry him beyond the immediate situation, a child is not able to see beyond his world. When his situation changes, he has no escape from the strange and unfamiliar world he confronts.

The main turning points in childhood, it seems, are transitions from world to world, from the womb to the world outside, from home to school, from one school to another, from one dwelling place to another. Each new and unfamiliar world is at once fascinating and dreadful to the child. Each time he is pulled out of a familiar world he feels alone in an unfamiliar world, gazing into the unknown. Each time he is plunged into a new world he has to learn a new relationship to the world. He has no steady relationship that can carry over from one world to another until later in life when he develops long-range interests and pursuits. Then he may find a lifelong pursuit that can carry him from one situation to another, a way of relating to any and every situation that comes along. Until then he is an immediate man and is at the mercy of the situation in which he finds himself.

A story is enacted each time the child goes from one world to another. In the beginning he is at home in a familiar world; then he becomes a stranger in a strange world; and then he is at home once again when the strange world becomes familiar. In the first instance, when he emerges from the womb into the world outside, he begins in a world of familiar darkness; then he is thrust into a world of dazzling and confusing light—"one big blooming buzzing confusion," as William James calls it;[8] and then the confusion gradually resolves for the child into a well-ordered universe. The story is like a story of creation in which there is first a darkness, then a chaos, and finally an ordered cosmos. We can imagine becoming stranded, however, in the middle state of chaos. "That confusion is the baby's universe," James says, "and the universe of all of us is still to a great extent such a confusion, potentially resolvable, and demanding to be resolved, but not yet actually resolved into parts."[9] If we are indeed stranded in the chaos, if the universe of all of us is still to a great extent such a confusion, then it will seem to us that we are in the midst of a creation story, a story that is still unfinished.

Actually, the confusion of which James speaks is not so much a continuous experience as a repeated experience. It occurs for the child each time his world changes; it occurs at the passing of childhood and the beginning of youth with the rise of sexuality and the dilemmas of love; it occurs at the passing of youth and the beginning of manhood with the rising sense of one's mortality and the dilemmas of death. It occurs really at each of the great turning points of life. When one is stranded in the moment of chaos during one of these changes, it can seem that one is living in a world in which evil goes unchecked, a world in which the monster has not yet been conquered. It can seem that the story of the world is unfinished. Looking at the whole series of turning points one has been through up to the present, one can see how at each point the confusion of the unfamiliar world was eventually resolved. Yet the fact that the strangeness and confusion have arisen again and again, each time on a wider scale, makes one think from this point of view too that one is in the midst of an unfinished story of creation.

The oldest stories of the world, the stories according to which a monster infesting the world is conquered, seem to describe a single cycle of human experience, a series of events that occur at each great turning point in human life when the chaos of a strange world is resolved into the order of a familiar universe. The Apache story of creation with which Geronimo begins his autobiography is just like one of these old stories from the first ages of history. In the beginning, he says, there was darkness on the earth. At that time "all creatures had the power of speech and were gifted with reason."[10] The birds led by the eagle wished to admit light into the darkness, but the beasts led by a nameless monster wished the darkness to remain. There was a great battle that ended when the eagle dropped an enormous stone upon the monster. Then the light came into the darkness. Man too had part in the struggle. A boy killed with arrows a dragon that had been devouring the children of men in the darkness, and the boy became the father of Geronimo's people.

All three phases of experience appear in the story: first the darkness like that of the womb from which the children of men must emerge if they are to thrive, then the chaos in which the birds and beasts are struggling, and then the well-ordered universe in which the monster has been killed by the eagle and the dragon has been killed by the boy. The story of creation that Augustine tells at the end of his autobiography, the story from Genesis, does not seem to describe these three phases. Coming as it does at the end of his autobiography, after he has described the great turning points of his life, the story seems to tell not what happens at any given turning point so much as what happens in the whole course of a life, what comes about through the whole series of turning points. It seems to say that the life story is a story of creation, that a man's life is a becoming in which he goes from nothingness to being. The story of creation is told, however, as though it were already accomplished. "And on the seventh day," we read, "God ended his work which he had made; and he rested on the seventh day from all his work which he had made."[11]

A man in his lifetime, nevertheless, finds himself still in the middle of becoming, still on his way from nothingness to being, as though the story of creation were still unfinished or as though it were a prophecy of something still to be consummated. The story Melville tells in *Moby Dick,* the story of a world in which the monster has not been overcome, seems to describe the experience of life in the middle of becoming, life in the middle between nothingness and being. It seems, in fact, to describe the experience of living in the middle of a cycle of human experience, living in the moment of chaos at one of the great turning points of life. Ahab, the protagonist of the story, dies in that moment, but Ishmael, the narrator, lives to tell the story. "And I only am escaped alone to tell Thee," Ishmael says at the end, quoting the Book of Job.[12] It is as though there were after all a moment following the moment of chaos, the moment, namely, in which the story is told. And that moment is the one when the fascinating and dreadful world man faces becomes a world in which he is at home.

The story of the world, that is, finally becomes the human thing that mediates between man and the unknown in the world, and the one who tells the story becomes the human being who is the mediator. Even if the story, like Melville's, is of a world where evil goes unchecked, a world where Moby Dick is at large, the story still has the power of mediation. The story of the world, it seems, is what finally brings order for the child into the "big blooming buzzing confusion" that he encounters on entering the world. He is learning the story of the world all the while he is learning the names of things, while he is learning about the earth and the sky and the living and the dead. He is learning it too in all the stories he hears. If some important person in his life, if his grandfather, for instance, is a great storyteller, the world of stories can become almost as important to him as the world of experience. The story world is like "the old moon in the new moon's arms" as the dark part of the moon is sometimes called. The child is like the new moon, but he holds the old moon in his arms. His experience and consciousness are the thin edge of a new world, but through stories he has access to the old world of human experience.

The ages of man's life are like the phases of the moon. When he is a child, his consciousness is like the thin edge of light and his unconsciousness like the darkened face of a new moon. When he is a youth, his consciousness waxes like a waxing moon. When he is a man, it is full like a full moon. When he is an old man, it wanes like a waning moon until it becomes once more like the thin edge of light on the face of a darkened moon. The ages of life, other than manhood perhaps, are all phases of partial consciousness, partial brightness like the phases of the moon other than the full, like the crescent moon, the half moon, the gibbous moon. A man has a relationship, though, to the dark as well as the bright part of his world, to the unconscious as well as the conscious realm of his life. His relationship to the dark part is like the earthshine, the earthlight that faintly illuminates the dark part of the moon and can be seen especially when the moon is crescent. As a child, when consciousness is small and unconsciousness is great, his relationship to the dark may be a fear and a wonder. As a youth, when consciousness is increasing, it may be a daring and a venture or, because the darkness is still greater than the light, it may be "adolescence's doubt (the common doom), then scepticism, then disbelief." As a man, when consciousness seems full, it may be a confidence and a clarity or, because the other side of a full moon is dark, it may be "manhood's pondering repose of If."

Whatever it is, the relationship to the dark means that the whole man and his whole world are present at each stage of his life, just as the entire moon, bright and dark, is present at each of its phases. It means that the man and even the old man is present already in the child and the youth. It means that the child and the youth live on in the man and the old man. The time before and after life is like the dark of the moon, the week when no moonlight appears in the nighttime sky. Near that week, just before and after it, one can see after twilight the whole face of the moon faintly illuminated by the earthshine. Near the beginning and the end of life too, through the eyes of the child and the old man, the child listening to the story and the grandfather telling the story, one can see the whole mystery of man faintly illuminated by the story of the world. "Children can be told anything—anything," Dostoevsky's Idiot says.[13] And they are indeed told everything when they are told the story of the world. Yet there are things about man that one does not see distinctly except through the eyes of youth and manhood, things that one sees when the story of the world becomes a story of love and a story of death.

## 2. *The Youth and the Story of Love*

To see with the eyes of youth and manhood is in a way to see more and in another way to see less than one can see with the eyes of childhood. Not seeing beyond his world, the child sees less. Not seeing beyond it, however, he sees it and thus sees more than the youth and the man who see beyond it.

"Adolescence's doubt (the common doom), then scepticism, then disbelief" seem to come from seeing beyond the moment, from seeing the uncertainty of the future. What takes the youth beyond the immediate situation is not his sexuality, the sexual maturity that has come with the age of puberty, so much as the dilemma of coming to terms with his sexuality, the dilemma of finding a relationship to his sexuality. How to be a man, how to be a woman, that is the dilemma a person confronts on reaching sexual maturity. Sex like death is at once fascinating and dreadful, it seems, and when it comes to its full strength in a person at puberty, he or she is forced to come to terms with it, to come to terms with manhood or womanhood. "A new life begins."[14] These are the words Dante finds in the "book of memory" where the story of his youth begins.

The new beginning one finds in the beginning of one's youth has something to do with the beginning of everything, with the origin and goal of life. Sexuality is not only fascinating but dreadful, it seems, for it is experienced as a terrible purpose at work in one's life, a purpose that is not personal but somehow impersonal in its aims, a purpose that looks to the species rather than the individual, to the reproduction of one's kind rather than to one's personal development. If we were to ask "Why do we fear our sexuality?" we would undoubtedly be told that we fear it because we have been taught to fear it, because we have learned to see it as fraught with moral danger. In reality, though, the fear seems to go well beyond merely learned fears. It is like the fear of death. We could be told also that we have been taught to fear death, that we fear it because we have learned to fear it. Yet death seems in fact to be inherently fearful. Actually, we fear both our sexuality and our mortality for the same reason, it seems, because they are forces within us that drive beyond all personal goals, that threaten our personal existence by leading beyond it.

There is a link of some kind between sexuality and mortality. Sex and death emerge at the same point in the story of evolution. Before that point there are only asexual organisms, increasing and multiplying but not dying unless they are killed. After that point there are male and female, mating and reproducing and dying. The link appears from the inside, from the inner experience of the linkage, in the story of love as it is told down through the ages. The tale of Gilgamesh is mainly the story of a man who comes to consciousness of his mortality, but it contains also the story of a man, Gilgamesh's friend and counterpart Enkidu, who comes to consciousness of his sexuality. The tale of Odysseus is the story of a man who overcomes the dread and the fascination of death but who overcomes at the same time the dread and the fascination of sexuality. Both Gilgamesh and Odysseus resist the lure of goddesses, the fascination of a divine sexuality which is somehow deadly to human beings. Dante's tale, on the other hand, is that of a man who follows his beloved into the land of the dead, a story like that of Orpheus and Eurydice. Only Dante does not seek, like Orpheus, to bring his beloved back from the dead but lets her lead him on to the highest love, "the love that moves the sun and the other stars."[15]

The terrible purpose one begins to experience within oneself within the rise of sexuality in youth may be this very love that moves the sun and the stars. One could see it that way in a world like Dante's where "God saw everything that he had made, and, behold, it was very good."[16] In a world like that of Gilgamesh or Odysseus, though, a world that had been hardly won from a monster of chaos, or in a world like ours where the monster seems still at large like Moby Dick, that purpose might appear to be something much more ambiguous and dangerous. The Ulysses of James Joyce, for example, loves a woman who is woman and yet simultaneously the dreadful and fascinating goddess, a Penelope who is also a Calypso. At the beginning of the story she is a Calypso holding him captive by his fascination for her, but in the end she is a Penelope welcoming him home with her love. It is her Yes to him, his being loved rather than being fascinated by her, that changes her from a goddess into a woman for him. "I asked him with my eyes to ask again yes," she says at the end, "and then he asked me would I yes to say yes my mountain flower and first I put my arms around him yes and drew him down to me so he could feel my breasts all perfume yes and his heart was going like mad and yes I said yes I will Yes."[17]

The Yes that comes to this Ulysses is a love that can be received only when one realizes that one is mortal and that one can never live with an immortal goddess. At puberty one becomes conscious of one's sexuality but not yet of one's mortality. The full awareness that one is mortal usually comes later, it seems, with the passing of youth, when one sees oneself losing one's youth. Thus the full story of love, from Homer's *Odyssey* to Joyce's *Ulysses,* is the story not of a youth but of a man. It is a story not only of sexuality but of mortality; the sense of mortality must intervene between the sense of sexuality and the Yes of love. All we can find in youth itself is the beginning of the story, the rise of sexuality and the encounter with its dread and fascination. Still, the intense awareness of sexuality and the dilemma into which it thrusts a person, how to be a man, how to be a woman, is enough by itself to lead beyond childhood and the immediate world to a new vision of things, a sense of the past, a sense of the future.

At first the new vision may be little more than "adolescence's doubt," an uncertainty about the past, an uncertainty about the future. A person will have had interests in childhood—for instance, enthusiasm for stories, for music, for the sea, and for ships and for sailing—that will have given him some sense of having personal goals. With the rise of sexuality in early adolescence, then, he will begin to feel a driving purpose within himself that tends to overshoot his personal goals, to carry him beyond everything that he personally intends to be and to do. After succumbing for a while to the new power of this drive, indulging in sexual play or in sexual fantasy, he may react against it and try to subdue it, fearing it without really knowing why he fears it. His attempt to conquer it, successful or unsuccessful as it may be, becomes a relationship to his sexuality that brings both his past and his future into doubt. He finds himself becoming serious about his past and his future in a way that his childhood enthusiasms never led him to be. He finds himself concerned about the role sexuality played in his childhood, concerned in a way that he had never been concerned during childhood itself; he finds himself concerned simultaneously about the role it is to play in his future, about living with another or living alone, about being happy or unhappy with another, about being happy or unhappy alone.

He looks about him, goes from one person to another, looking for someone who is happy, encountering unhappiness as it seems to him all around him. He looks for some purpose in life, some personal purpose, that will be as powerful and consuming as the impersonal purpose, the driving force of sexuality that he feels within him. He looks for a personal purpose that will be equal to or greater than the impersonal purpose. It is at this point in his life that he is most readily attracted to an ideal of greatness or of holiness, to an ideal that requires great personal sacrifice as the price of great personal significance. The impersonal force within him driving beyond his personal goals and threatening his personal existence by leading beyond it makes his personal goals seem too small and his personal existence too insignificant. So he looks for greater goals and greater significance. Also, the power of the impersonal purpose he feels within gives him a taste of what a powerful purpose can be, how it drives against all odds, reaching out toward its object no matter how distant and inaccessible the object may be, how it is its own necessity, its own motivating force, and does not require any ulterior motive.

To be a great man, to be a holy man, these are the only worthwhile goals, it seems to him. Although he has not yet come to that later point in life when it can appear that one will never achieve the things one has always hoped to achieve, he may have some doubts even at this point as to whether he will really ever attain greatness or holiness. He may resolve the doubts by deciding to spend his life striving for greatness or holiness, thinking that even if he does not attain them, a life spent striving for them is much more significant than one spent striving for petty or mundane goals. To make the highest possibility of human life one's goal gives one's life an incomparable unity, even if one never actually attains it but spends one's entire life on the way to it. That highest possibility, whether it is conceived as greatness or holiness, can be felt immediately as a purpose, a purpose that is personal and yet altogether as powerful and consuming as the impersonal drive one feels within. It is something for which no sacrifice seems too great, even the sacrifice of one's sexual desires. It is in fact something to which, it seems, one can harness the power of one's sexuality. It is, Freud would say, the sexual desire itself in a new guise.

"My interest," Freud says in his autobiography, "after making a lifelong detour through the natural sciences, medicine and psychotherapy, returned to the cultural problems which had fascinated me long before, when I was a youth scarcely old enough for thinking."[18] The "cultural problems" of which he speaks are two, civilization and religion. We could associate them with the two ideals of which we are speaking, greatness and holiness. The route Freud took may be an archetypal one: a youthful fascination with greatness and holiness, then a lifelong detour, and then finally a return to the interests of one's youth. During the detour one finds what one thinks is the real substance of one's youthful ideals. Freud himself, for example, thought that the substance was sexuality. In the end, nevertheless, and in spite of having reduced one's ideals to "nothing but . . . ," one is still fascinated by them.

Why should there be a lifelong detour? Why, first of all, would a man depart from his original ideals and why, then, having departed from them, would he return to them once more? Perhaps it is because the ideals partake of the ambiguity, the dread and the fascination of sexuality itself. "I had a strong intuition," Jung says, speaking of Freud, "that for him sexuality was a sort of *numinosum*. . . . Sexuality evidently meant more to Freud than to other people."[19] The *numi-*

*nosum*, the divine or the holy, we could say, is the dreadful and the fascinating. Sexuality was this for Freud, it seems, but if what we have been saying is true, it is this for other people as well. One encounters the holy—the dreadful and the fascinating—in different guises in the course of one's life, earlier in the guise of sex and later in the guise of death. One approaches it like Moses approaching the burning bush, fascinated by a bush that is burning and not consumed and at the same time terrified by the power that can burn without consuming.

There is something wanting, it is true, in this initial relationship with sexuality. As long as sexuality is numinous, as long as it is dreadful and fascinating, it is not yet fully human. The same is true of death. As long as death is felt as a dreadful and fascinating power outside, a power that one can wield and that can be wielded against one, a force that will ultimately strike one down from the outside, then death is not yet human, is not yet seen and felt as human mortality. Some kind of odyssey thus is necessary in which one goes from divine to human sexuality and from the power of death to the mortality of man. Somehow God must become man, the holy must become human. First there is an encounter with love, love in the form of numinous sexuality. Then there is an encounter with death, death in the form of a numinous power threatening one from the outside. Then there is a realization that one is mortal and a sensing of the link between one's mortality and one's sexuality. At this point one becomes fully conscious of being human and is ready at last for a second encounter with love, for the consent to one's humanity which is the Yes of love.

What for another man would be a life experience becomes

for Freud a lifework. We can see in the story of his lifework, as he tells it, first the encounter with sexuality when he makes the "pleasure principle" the basis of his theory and practice of psychoanalysis, then the encounter with death later on when he writes *Beyond the Pleasure Principle* and introduces alongside sexuality "an instinct of death or destruction which works in silence."[20] Both sex and death, however, seem to remain numinous for him, dreadful and fascinating. Neither of them ever seems to become something fully human. They remain powers at work within man, dark and transcendent powers. The Yes of love, the loving consent to sexuality and mortality that renders them fully human, never quite occurs.

When one becomes fully conscious of sexuality and mortality and yet does not fully consent to them, one has the feeling of being forced into something against one's will. One feels plunged into life and time, forced to be at the point in life where one is. It is as if one had been hurled from timelessness into time. "We have learnt that unconscious mental processes are in themselves 'timeless,'" Freud says. "This means in the first place that they are not ordered temporally, that time does not change them in any way and that the idea of time cannot be applied to them."[21] Sexuality and mortality both, we could say, are relatively unconscious processes in childhood and do not affect one's consciousness of time as they do afterwards in youth and manhood. Time, or the developed sense of time, seems to come about as sexuality and mortality emerge into consciousness, sexuality with the coming of youth and mortality with the passing of youth.

There are sexual metamorphoses during childhood, to be

sure, the oral and anal and genital phases of which Freud speaks, but sexuality does not seem yet to be the conscious process it becomes at puberty. When I remember my childhood, I can find there encounters with sex, even encounters with death. When I see with the eyes I had as a child, though, what I see, what fills my awareness is the world, a fascinating and dreadful world of which sex and death are only parts. There is time in that world, past and present and future, but only the present is real, not the past or the future. The past is the no longer; the future is the not yet. Thus there is a kind of timelessness about things in the world, almost as if the present were without past and future. Things are like people in a room or animals in a forest. They do not appear yet as things that belong to a life and must enter into it, each in turn, each in its time, as they do when sexuality begins to rise in consciousness. Nor do they appear as things that must pass away, each again in turn, each again in its time, as they do when mortality begins to rise.

"Grasping time is tantamount to freeing oneself from the present," Piaget says in *The Child's Conception of Time*.[22] The child gradually learns to discern time, Piaget says, to discern past and present and future, and to reckon time. Yet the child is not thereby freed from the present, we could say, for he still lives largely in the moment. He learns about time from adults, but his living does not catch up with his thinking until puberty. Then a change takes place in his living that leads to a new sense of time. He becomes concerned about the future and the past, and they become real for him in a way that they never were before. Now that he is a youth rather than a child, sexuality is strong in him and forces him, though he may long to flee back to the moment, to come to terms with his future and his past, to come to terms with his life as a whole. A young man or young woman is freed from the present, but the freedom is not a pleasant one. It is rather a dilemma, how to be a man, how to be a woman. The things of the world become things of life, but life then becomes a dilemma. Everything belongs to one's life, it seems, and everything must somehow enter into it.

It is the entrance of sexuality into one's life that gives one the sense of things entering one's life. There is no sense as yet of things passing from one's life other than a rather vague one that comes from the passing of one's childhood. It is later on with the passing of one's youth that the sense of one's mortality begins to grow, the sense that all the things of life must pass. At that point, one's sense of time expands once again, reaching the boundaries of one's lifetime, death in the future and birth in the past, and by reaching the boundaries it comes to the prospect of the time that lies beyond, the great time that encompasses one's lifetime. Here again one meets a dilemma, the dilemma of coming to terms with the great time, the dilemma of coming to terms with death. One's vision of time is always expanding, from the child's vision of the moment to the youth's vision of the lifetime to the man's vision of the great time. While one's vision of time is expanding, though, one seems to be losing one's hold on eternity. One loses first the timelessness of the child, then the inexhaustible time of the youth. One ends with the mortal existence of the man.

## 3. *The Man and the Story of Death*

A man's vision of time, when it first comes to him in the passing of youth, is a lonely and foreboding prospect. It is like daybreak at sea. Dana describes that in *Two Years Before the Mast*:

> There is something in the first grey streaks stretching along the eastern horizon and throwing an indistinct light upon the face of the deep, which combines with the boundlessness and unknown depth of the sea around you, and gives one a feeling of loneliness, of dread, and of melancholy foreboding which nothing else in nature can give.[23]

One's vision of time is like that too at first. It is a daybreak that reveals the horizon of one's life, that suggests the boundlessness and the unknown depth of time encompassing one's life. It fills one with loneliness and dread and melancholy foreboding.

The loneliness is like that of Ahab gazing into sea and sky: "Let me look into a human eye; it is better than to gaze into sea or sky, better than to gaze upon God." Looking out over time, one feels alone, gazing into an inhuman expanse, into something that far exceeds one's lifetime. One longs to look rather into a human eye, to see the vast expanse reduced there to tiny human dimensions. The experience is that of unmediated existence. There is nothing human to stand between one and the unknown, and here the unknown takes the form of the immense ocean of time. One longs to see the vision of time in another human eye, to see it seen rather than to see it, to let it become human through the mediation of another human being. This is what we have been trying to do throughout this book so far. We have been looking for the vision of time in the eyes of former men and contemporary men. We have been looking for the vision of the moment and the vision of life that precede the full vision of time in the eyes of childhood and youth.

Everywhere we have found something of the loneliness, the dread, the melancholy foreboding that one experiences when one faces time by oneself. It is not lonely, though, or dreadful or melancholy or foreboding to see those things in another human eye. The mediation of other human beings seems to take away somehow the inhuman quality of time. We have called the approaches of former men a "quest of life" or a "return home" or a "journey through the otherworld." We have called that of our contemporaries an "exploration of this world." What should we call our own approach? Perhaps a "search for mediation." Perhaps it is by searching for mediation, by going from mediator to mediator, by looking into many human eyes, that one goes in quest of life, returns home, journeys through the otherworld, explores this world.

The classic autobiographies of modern times, those of Rousseau, Wordsworth, and Goethe, can all be read as accounts of the search for mediation. Rousseau's *Confessions,* like his later *Reveries of a Solitary Walker,* describes a man living in a state of unmediated existence, a solitary man. Wordsworth's *Prelude* describes such a man, too, but it describes one who seeks always to deal with time through the mediation of his own memory, who seeks to put himself as child and as youth between time and himself as man. Goethe's *Poetry and Truth* describes the original of Faust, a man who seeks always to put woman (the "eternal womanly," as he says[24]) between himself and time, to put woman transfigured by poetry between himself and the truth of his life.

One may find oneself doing all of these things. One may find oneself living like Rousseau in a state of unmediated existence, feeling it to be at times a state of unhappy loneliness, at times a state of happy solitude. One may find oneself making use of memory like Wordsworth, as we have been doing in this chapter, to see things with the eyes of the child or the youth, to place oneself as child or youth between time and oneself as man. One may find oneself trying like Goethe to place woman between oneself and time, or more generally to place other persons between oneself and time, and going in search of mediation from one person to another. Is the search for mediation, one wonders, merely an escape from time? Does it amount, as Camus puts it in *A Happy Death*, to "taking refuge in humanity"?[25]

Let us imagine a man who goes in search of mediation. Say he starts from a situation of unmediated existence. Say he succeeds in finding mediation. Say he goes from one mediator to another. Say he always comes back, though, to unmediated existence. Like Ahab, he longs to look into a human eye, but as soon as he looks there, he turns away again to gaze once more into the sea and sky. He does not escape, therefore, from time. His vision of time, nonetheless, may be profoundly changed. He starts with a simple consciousness of mortality, an awareness of the things of life, how they enter his life and how they must pass again from his life. His dread at this spectacle makes him long to look into a human eye and see it seen rather than see it. His fascination with it, though, draws him back to gaze at it again and again. Going back and forth between mediated and unmediated existence, he may come in the end to see not only the things of life but also his relationship to the things of his life. He may progress through adventures of the spirit from a simple consciousness of mortality to a consciousness of spirit.

Say the first person who succeeds in mediating between him and time is a joyous and selfless person, a woman who accepts her death with joy, a man who gives his life to the service of others. Seeing time in the eyes of such a person, the man we are imagining is amazed that such joy and selflessness are possible and he is ashamed at his own self-centered life, at how he is unwilling to say Yes to his own death, at how he seems never to pursue anything other than his own happiness. Yet it is the self, he reflects, that sacrifices the self. The word "selflessness" is not really an accurate name for the self-sacrificing life that he is admiring. "The self," Kierkegaard says, "is a relation which relates itself to its own self."[26] To sacrifice itself is a way of relating to itself. When a man encounters self-sacrifice, when he sees a man or a woman sacrifice themselves, he is encountering what we have called "spirit." He is encountering not one of the things of life like sexuality or mortality but a relationship to the things, in fact, "a relation which relates itself to its own self."

Self-centeredness, too, is "a relation which relates itself to its own self," a self seeking itself, just as self-sacrifice is a self giving itself. Say the second person who succeeds in mediating between time and the man we are envisioning is self-centered like him but more passionately so. Such a person can be very attractive. Somehow the person who is absorbed in self has a kind of ascendancy over others. "One person's narcissism has a great attraction for those others who have renounced part of their own narcissism and are seeking after object-love," Freud says. "The charm of a child lies to a great extent in his narcissism, his self-sufficiency and in-

accessibility."[27] Narcissism, being absorbed in self like
Narcissus, who fell in love with the image of himself reflected in the water, is very fascinating to others because it
seems to reveal a beautiful and fascinating self. Looking into
the eyes of such a person, a man sees time only insofar as it
reflects that person's image. When he comes back to himself
and gazes directly again into the ocean of time, he may see
his own image there.

When one sees one's own image reflected on the waters of
time, when one sees everything in terms of oneself, there is
danger that the boundary between self and other will disappear, that one will fall into madness, that one will lose
oneself. We can imagine Narcissus drowning as he tries to
embrace his image in the water. Say the third person who
comes to mediate between the man we are supposing and
time is indeed mad. Say the madness consists in losing the
self in the other. "You and I, are we not the same?" such a
person might say, ". . . sometimes I cannot tell myself from
other people."[28] Or say it consists in losing the self in
things. "That's the rain. I could be the rain," a mad girl once
said. "That chair—that wall. I could be the wall. It's a terrible thing for a girl to be a wall."[29] The man we are imagining, let us say, is fascinated by such a person. He knows that
she is mad, but he is fascinated nonetheless. There is some
kind of profound truth, he sees, in her madness. If the human spirit is a relationship to the things of life, there is nothing to stop it from being a relationship to all the things in the
world. Everything in the world enters a life.

What is there then to stop one from falling into madness,
from drowning, from losing oneself in everything? To relate
to the things of life is spirit; to relate to the relationship is

self. The self is "a relation which relates itself to its own self." To go beyond the self one must learn to relate to the things. To see beyond one's own reflection and hear beyond one's own echo, one would have to look and listen in such a way as to let something other than oneself appear. "Wherever we are, what we hear is mostly noise," the composer John Cage says. "When we ignore it, it disturbs us. When we listen to it, we find it fascinating."[30] Something similar could be said of seeing. When we ignore what is before our eyes, it disturbs us. When we see it, we find it fascinating. Say the fourth person who comes to mediate between the man we are envisioning and time is one who truly sees and hears. Looking through the eyes, listening through the ears of such a person, a man begins to see and hear what he has hitherto ignored, what has hitherto been only a disturbance in his life.

The things he learns to see and hear are wonderfully indifferent toward him. They neither love him nor hate him; they leave him completely free. He enjoys a freedom of spirit, seeing and hearing, going from one thing to another. The persons he has met so far have left him free too, each one of them simply mediating between him and time. Say he comes at last, though, to meet a person who falls in love with him, who will not merely mediate between him and time, merely be transparent for him, but loves him and wishes to be loved by him in return. Now he truly encounters self, the "relation which relates itself to its own self," the self of another person. He has already encountered self-sacrifice and self-centeredness, it is true, loss of self in the other and seeing and hearing the other as distinct from the self, but the selves he has encountered up till now have not included him in their circle. The circle of the self is closed, but now, meeting one who loves him and wishes to be loved by him in return, he is caught in the circle of another person's self. A woman who loves him relates to his self but wants that self to relate back again to her own self; she says Yes to him but wants him to say Yes to her in return.

If he does say Yes in return, then each one's self becomes included within the other's self, each self relates to itself by way of the other. The woman took a risk in loving him, the risk of losing herself somehow if he should not return her love. Say he sees the risk she has taken and sees also that he is taking the same risk himself, that if the relationship should be destroyed, he would somehow lose himself. Say it is in fact destroyed; she is taken away from him by some eventuality. Now he faces time alone once more. Having related to himself by way of another, he finds it difficult to relate to himself again in his aloneness. He feels as though he had no more self. Once the circle of self has been opened to include another person, it seems that it can never be satisfactorily closed again.

There is nothing but spirit left, it seems, his relationship to the things of life. "Spirit is the self,"[31] Kierkegaard says, but that is true only so long as the relationship can come back upon itself, only so long as the circle of the self can be closed. When the circle has been opened, there is the beginning of an infinite spiral. Spirit still comes back upon itself through consciousness; the relationship to things is a conscious one and to that extent it relates to itself. It does not come back upon itself through consent, though; the broken circle does not consent to its own brokenness. It is like a spiral, therefore, always coiling back upon itself but never meeting itself. If the broken circle were to consent to its own brokenness, it would be mended; the circle of the self would be closed again. If a man were to consent to the life of the spirit after seeing it lead to the breaking of his self, then his self would be restored to him. The act of consenting would be the closing of the circle.

When the circle is broken, a man feels that he is sundered, sundered from himself, from others, from God. "As I write this a madman is howling in the next room," Nietzsche wrote from the insane asylum, "and I am howling with him inside of me, howling for my lost integrity, sundered from God, Man and myself, shattered in body, mind and spirit, yearning for two clasped hands to usher in the great miracle— the unity of my being."[32] It does indeed seem to take two clasped hands to close the circle of the human spirit. Nietzsche was speaking of love, the failure of his relationship with the woman he loved, Lou Salomé. He had succeeded in his lifework; he had created Zarathustra much as Goethe created Faust; he had created a self of poetry, but he had lost his self of truth. A man's lifework is always something like this, the shaping of another self, a self that can withstand time and death. His true self, however, is endangered by the self he has created. When he has spent his life fashioning a particular image of his being, he may break and shatter rather than become something else.

It may be that he is required to become something else, that his part in the story of mankind is other than what he thought it to be. His lifework from the viewpoint of others is his way of mediating between them and time, while from his own point of view it is the making of an enduring self. He may take responsibility for others; he may struggle for them; he may take risks for them; he may suffer for them; he

may die for them. Whatever he does, he faces time somehow
for them, while for himself he fashions a self that can stand
in the face of time and death. A broken and shattered self too,
though, can mediate between others and time; it can refract
time as the broken pieces of glass refract light in a kaleido-
scope. Time faced directly seems inhuman; reflected by an
integral self it seems human and even tame; refracted by a
broken self it seems wild and yet human. What a man is to
others can succeed, therefore, while what he is to himself
fails. He can still successfully mediate between time and
others when the circle of his own spirit has been broken.

Closing the circle of the human spirit is a different quest
than searching for mediation. The object of a search for
mediation is to find a relationship to time and death. The object of closing the circle of the spirit is to find a relation to
the relationship itself. The one quest may lead into the other.
A man may set out to find someone to mediate between him
and time and end, like Nietzsche, "yearning for two clasped
hands to usher in the great miracle—the unity of my being."
If he ends this way, he is likely to feel that he has regressed,
that he has turned back from the man's task of relating to
time and death to the youth's task of relating to life and love.
"Not art, not science, not philosophy," Nietzsche wrote, "but
falling in love has usurped the whole landscape of my
foundered being."[33] To the degree that a man seeks a relationship to sexuality, he is indeed returning to an unfinished
task of youth. To the degree that he seeks a relationship to
spirit, however, he is facing a task that he has never really
faced before.

Spirit seems to become an issue at a certain time of life
much as sexuality and mortality do, though like them it

pervades the whole life from beginning to end. Sexuality becomes an issue with the passing of childhood and the beginning of youth; mortality becomes an issue with the passing of youth and the beginning of manhood; spirit becomes an issue in the midst of manhood. If the emergence of death into one's life is like daybreak at sea, an experience of loneliness and dread and melancholy foreboding, the emergence of spirit is like the passing of daybreak into what Dana calls "the ordinary monotonous sea day."[34] The restlessness of the human spirit makes the prospect of life opening up before one all the way to death seem monotonous. The only cure for the restlessness, it seems, is consent, a Yes to the life of the spirit, a Yes to the restlessness itself. The restlessness is like the unquiet of the sea, the constant motion of the waves. To be willingly restless is to be at rest; to be willingly unquiet is to be quiet. It is like a calm in which the sea becomes transparent to its depths.

A willing restlessness is still restless, though, a willing unquiet still unquiet. The most one can say is that it is a rest in restlessness, a quiet in unquiet. It was on a clear and tranquil day at sea that Ahab uttered the words we quoted, "Let me look into a human eye; it is better than to gaze into sea or sky, better than to gaze upon God." Ahab, to be sure, was not at rest in his restlessness nor quiet in his unquiet. Yet even a man who is willingly restless, willingly unquiet, could still desire to look into a human eye. Consenting to the restlessness of the spirit amounts to consenting to the adventures of the spirit and that would include all three of the things that Ahab names, looking into a human eye, gazing into the sea and sky, and gazing upon God.

At each stage of life something unknown comes one's

way: in childhood it is the world, in puberty it is sexuality, in the passing of youth it is mortality, and in the midst of manhood it is spirit. "Gazing into the sea and sky," we could say, is the adventure of coming to terms with the unknown at each stage. First the unknown enters one's consciousness, and then it becomes a matter for one's consent. When it first enters one's consciousness it is dreadful and fascinating; it is holy, that is, and the "gazing into the sea and sky" is a "gazing upon God." The world is dreadful and fascinating to the child, sexuality is so to the youth, death is so to the man, and spirit itself is ultimately so. When one consents to the unknown, however, it seems to lose its dread and fascination, to lose its divinity and become human. The world becomes familiar; sexuality becomes one's manhood or womanhood, death becomes one's mortality, and spirit becomes one's self. The difficulty of consenting, though, is that one cannot bring oneself to say Yes to the unknown until it seems human, but it does not seem human until one says Yes.

"Looking into a human eye" is the way through the dilemma, the way from consciousness to consent. For when one looks into a human eye instead of gazing directly into the sea and sky, instead of gazing directly upon God, one sees the unknown reduced to tiny human dimensions, one sees it lose its dread and fascination. The child, for example, when he sees the world through the eyes of the storyteller, sees the world in all its dreadful and fascinating mystery, and yet feels it to be human and familiar. It is like looking at a beautiful image of something ugly. One sees the ugliness and yet one sees it through the medium of beauty. So it is with one's sexuality and mortality too. Seen directly, they appear to be wild and dark powers at work in one's life; seen through the eyes of another they can appear to be integral aspects of one's humanity. With one's own eyes as a child, one sees the things of the world in all their strangeness; as a youth, one sees that each of them belongs to one's life and must enter into it; as a man, one sees that each in its time passes away again from one's life. Looking through the eyes of another one sees not only the things but one's relationship to the things. It is like actually looking into the pupil of another's eye and seeing there the tiny image of oneself set against the tiny background of sea and sky.

When one looks into a human eye, one finds that one can consent, can say Yes to the things of life, to the sea and sky in the background, and can say Yes also to the relationship to things, to oneself in the foreground. A Yes is required of one, it seems, at each stage of life. There is a task at each stage that begins with a consciousness and ends with a consent. The world emerges into consciousness, then sexuality, then mortality, and then spirit. At each stage, one's task is accomplished when one makes one's way through to consent. If one does not reach that point, the task remains unfinished and carries into the next stage of life. If one does succeed in consenting, then the thing that has emerged into consciousness becomes something human. It loses its divine and uncanny quality and becomes part of one's humanity. When that happens, one comes up against God. It is as though the Yes were a Yes to someone and not merely a Yes to something, a Yes to God and not merely a Yes to the world, to sexuality, to mortality, to spirit. God becomes God in the moment when man becomes man.

# NOTES TO CHAPTER TWO

1. Herman Melville, *Moby Dick,* ed. by Luther S. Mansfield and Howard P. Vincent (New York, Hendricks House, 1952), Chap. 132, p. 535.

2. Sergei Aksakoff, *Years of Childhood,* tr. by J. D. Duff (London, Oxford University Press, 1923).

3. Geronimo, *Geronimo: His Own Story,* ed. by S. M. Barrett (New York, Dutton, 1970), p. 61. First published in 1906.

4. Genesis 1:1f. Augustine, *Confessions,* XI–XIII. Cf. my book *A Search for God in Time and Memory* (New York, Macmillan, 1970), pp. 55ff., 169f.

5. C. G. Jung, *Memories, Dreams, Reflections,* ed. by Aniela Jaffé, tr. by Richard and Clara Winston (New York, Vintage, 1965), p. 171.

6. Melville, op. cit., Chap. 114, p. 486; he speaks there of going through this cycle not only once but again and again.

7. William Butler Yeats, *Autobiographies* (London, Macmillan, 1955), p. 5.

8. William James, *Psychology* (Cleveland, World, 1948), p. 16.

9. Ibid.

10. Geronimo, loc. cit.

11. Genesis 2:2. Augustine, *Confessions,* XIII. 35ff; here Augustine speaks of the sabbath of eternal life, and that has the effect of placing the ending of the creation and God's rest at the end of life and time.

12. Melville, op. cit., Epilogue, p. 567. Cf. Job 1:15ff.

13. Fyodor Dostoevsky, *The Idiot,* tr. by Constance Garnett (New York, Dell, 1959), p. 90.

14. Dante, *Vita Nuova,* I.

15. Dante, *Paradiso,* XXXIII, 145.

16. Genesis 1:31.

17. James Joyce, *Ulysses* (New York, Modern Library, 1961), closing words (p. 768).

18. Sigmund Freud, *An Autobiographical Study*, tr. by James Strachey (New York, Norton, 1963), p. 137.
19. Jung, op. cit., pp. 150f.
20. Freud, op. cit., p. 109.
21. Freud, *Beyond the Pleasure Principle*, tr. by James Strachey (New York, Bantam Books, 1967), p. 54.
22. Jean Piaget, *The Child's Conception of Time*, tr. by A. J. Pomerans (New York, Basic Books, 1969), p. 259.
23. Richard Dana, *Two Years Before the Mast* (Cleveland and New York, World, 1946), Chap. 2, p. 22.
24. Goethe, *Faust*, Part II. 12110, "Das Ewig-Weibliche." Cf. *Goethes Faust*, ed. by Erich Trunz (Hamburg, Wegner, 1960), p. 364.
25. Albert Camus, *A Happy Death*, tr. by Richard Howard (New York, Knopf, 1972), p. 113.
26. Sören Kierkegaard, *Sickness unto Death*, tr. by Walter Lowrie (Garden City, Doubleday, 1954), p. 146.
27. Freud, "On Narcissism," in *Collected Papers*, ed. by Joan Riviere, Vol. IV (London, Hogarth Press, 1956), p. 46.
28. Norman Brown, *Love's Body* (New York, Vintage, 1966), p. 160.
29. Ibid.
30. John Cage, *Silence* (Cambridge, Mass., M.I.T. Press, 1969), p. 3.
31. Kierkegaard, loc. cit.
32. F. W. Nietzsche, *My Sister and I* (New York, Bridgehead Books, 1951), p. 233.
33. Ibid., p. 42.
34. Dana, loc. cit.

# THREE

# The Moment and the Story of God

What is man apart from the things of his life, apart from loving and fighting and dying? A child is an image of what man is before the things of life have entered his life. An old man is an image of what man is when all the things have passed. Consider, for instance, the old man in Ernest Hemingway's story, *The Old Man and the Sea*. "Everything about him was old except his eyes and they were the same color as the sea and were cheerful and undefeated."[1]

His eyes were "the same color as the sea." It is as though he had a relationship with the sea, a kinship with it. He lived by struggling with the sea, and he had gone for many days without catching a fish. His eyes were cheerful, though, and undefeated. How could the sea defeat him when he was kin to it, when he had a secret relationship with it? To defeat him, it would have to defeat itself. He is an image of man and the sea an image of the unknown. A man has a relationship with the unknown, the old man seems to say, a kinship with it. Although he spends his life struggling with the unknown, wrestling with it as Jacob is supposed to have wrestled with God, he is not really defeated. His eyes can be cheerful and undefeated even after a lifetime of apparently futile struggle. There is something about him that is independent of time and age. It is his relationship with the unknown. When all else is gone, the unknown remains and his relationship to it remains.

How does a man relate to the unknown? How is he akin to it? He relates to it, the old man seems to say, by struggling with it, by wrestling with it. He encounters the unknown at each crisis of his life. How he responds to it in the crises determines what his relationship with it shall be. Really he spends his whole life establishing a relationship with the unknown. There is a kinship he has with it, nevertheless, from the beginning, before he has struggled with it or responded to it in any way, and that is his capacity to relate to the unknown, his capacity to struggle with it. A child is an image of man in that bare capacity, that original kinship. An old man is an image of man in his actual relationship with the unknown, established through a lifetime of struggle. A man's eyes are the same color as the unknown from the beginning. They can be cheerful and undefeated in the end.

Man's struggle with the unknown, his wrestling with God, is the human experience that seems to underlie the great religions. Each meeting with the unknown is a moment in which man enacts his relationship with the unknown. From the other side, the side of the unknown, each meeting is an episode in the story of God. There are three meetings, it seems, three episodes. The first is the meeting that occurs when a man comes up against one of the crises of his life. The second is when he goes into solitude to come to grips with the unknown. The third is when he returns from solitude to meet the unknown among men. One leads to another. The crisis leads to the withdrawal and the withdrawal leads to the return. Let us examine each episode in turn and see what happens to man and what happens to the unknown.

## 1. The Crisis and the Withdrawal

We could imagine three men meeting the unknown in these three moments of crisis and withdrawal and return. That is what Dostoevsky did in his tale of the three brothers Karamazov. Dimitri, the eldest of the three brothers, meets the unknown at a crisis: he faces suffering, being falsely accused of murdering his father, and hopes through suffering to become a new man. Ivan, the next in age, meets it in a withdrawal: he goes within himself but finds in his solitude only doubt and despair. Alyosha, the youngest, meets it on a return: he returns to the world from the monastery and runs out into the night and kisses the earth. The three are brothers, though, almost three aspects of one and the same man. Let us imagine one man, therefore, who goes through all three episodes, who meets the unknown at a crisis, then withdraws to meet it in solitude, and finally returns to meet it among men.

If we were to imagine three men instead of one, we would have to see the one who withdraws from the world as being somehow at odds with the other two and needing to be reunited with them. "Love Ivan," Dimitri says at the end to Alyosha.[2] Dimitri says this who has never left the world, and he says it to Alyosha who has returned to the world. Ivan, on the other hand, has rejected the world. "It's not that I don't accept God, you must understand," he tells Alyosha.

"It's the world created by him I don't and cannot accept."[3] Now, if we imagine one man instead of three, we will have to envision this conflict going on within him. The reconciliation too will have to take place within him. That changes things, for it is no longer enough for him to love the man who withdraws. He is that man. If there is to be a reconciliation now, it seems he must love that part of himself that wants to withdraw. He must love the withdrawal itself.

There is a hatred of the world, a No, in the withdrawal just as there is a love of the world, a Yes, in the return. If there is to be a reconciliation within him, it seems he will have to love his own hatred. He will have to say Yes to his own No. Sylvia Plath has it in her autobiographical novel *The Bell Jar* that "to the person in the bell jar, blank and stopped as a dead baby, the world itself is the bad dream."[4] There is hatred of the world here—the waking world is the nightmare rather than the world of sleep. It is so to the person in the bell jar, the person who withdraws. Now, that person may return and come to love the world that he hated. What happens then to the person who withdrew and to his hatred? If he and it disappear, then we have simply a man who once hated the world and now loves it, a man who once withdrew and now has returned. If, however, the person who withdraws lives on in the person who returns, if the one's No lives on in the other's Yes, then we have a man who has struggled with the unknown and has not given up the struggle.

He is like the old man who spent his life struggling with the sea, whose eyes "were the same color as the sea and were cheerful and undefeated." There is a unity in his life because at each stage, crisis and withdrawal and return, he has met the unknown. It is the unknown that gives unity to his life in all its phases, and it is his relationship to the unknown more than his relationship to the world that makes him what he is. What shape, then, let us ask, does the unknown take when he meets it? How does it appear in a crisis, in a withdrawal, in a return?

"I've found in myself a new man," Dimitri tells Alyosha. "A new man has risen up in me. He was hidden in me, but would never have come to the surface, if it hadn't been for this blow from heaven."[5] The crisis he calls a "blow from heaven." The unknown is the "new man" that is hidden in him and that comes to the surface in the crisis. In another way the unknown is the God that strikes the blow. There seems to be some kind of affinity between the two, between the unknown within and the unknown without, between the new man and the God. The new man, according to Dostoevsky's story, is a man of spirit who is hidden in a man of flesh and who emerges when Dimitri is refined by suffering. Before the "blow from heaven" his life is shaped by passion, passion as emotion. After the blow his life is shaped by passion in another sense, passion as suffering. He becomes "a suffering consciousness."[6] His God is the God of a suffering consciousness, a God of suffering.

Let us imagine rather a different man, almost the opposite of Dimitri, a man let us say who lives the life of the spirit but is lacking instead in the life of the flesh. Spirit, as we have been conceiving it, consists of a man's relationship to the things of his life; flesh, we could say, consists of the things themselves, the things that must enter his life and then pass again from it. If we conceive spirit and flesh this way, then one cannot be without the other. There cannot be a relationship without things to relate to nor can there be things without relating to them. Still, it is possible for one or the other to dominate a life. There can be a man like Dimitri whose passion is for the things of life and whose life tends therefore to be dominated by flesh. And there can be a man like the one we are now starting to envision who cares more about his relationship to the things than about the things themselves and whose life tends therefore to be dominated by spirit.

There is a season for each of the things of life, "a time to weep and a time to laugh . . . a time to get and a time to lose . . . a time to love and a time to hate."[7] A man whose care is for the things of life will be subject to the seasons, will laugh when it is the time for laughter and weep when it is the time for weeping. A man whose care is rather for his relationship to the things may try to cultivate a relationship that will hold steady through all the changes of season. He may try to cultivate an inner peace, for example, that will hold steady through the time for weeping and the time for laughter. His peace may be like the "archaic smile," the smile that one seems to see on the faces of the most ancient Greek sculptures. It may be only an apparent joy just as the archaic smile is only an apparent smile that comes from a way of carving the human face with high cheekbones and slightly upturned lips. His peace, instead of being a perpetual state of joy, may be only a steady relationship, steady through joy and sorrow, unchanging as a sculptured face.

Behind his archaic smile there may be a history of turmoil, of lust and rage and effort to escape from lust and rage. The steady relationship may represent a victory over the ups and downs of emotion. He may seem after he has achieved it to lack passion. Yet he may be passionate in fact, passionate about his relationship, passionate with all the energy he once expended in alternating emotions. There is something missing nevertheless. Emotions come in pairs of opposites: love and hatred, desire and disgust, joy and sorrow, fear and daring, hope and despair. So they have each their own time, and a man whose care is the things of life will be carried from one to another, from opposite to opposite. When a man has achieved a steady relationship to the things of his life, he may no longer be carried back and forth, but the occasions for the opposite emotions, the seasons for the various things of life, will still occur in his life.

If the man of flesh like Dimitri has hidden within him a man of spirit, the man of spirit will have hidden within him a man of flesh, a man who responds to the things of life in their seasons. Say he has the things he values most—hope, peace, friends, insight—and say he has them and cultivates them through his steady relationship to the things of life. Say he lacks intimacy, though, say he lacks any real intimacy with another person. Lacking intimacy, he never gets caught up in love and hatred, getting and losing, weeping and laughter. He never gets caught up in the things of life and their seasons. There will be something or someone in him nonetheless that wants intimacy. There will be a man of flesh in him that wants love though it means also hatred, that wants getting though it means also losing, that wants laughter though it means also weeping. The man of flesh in him may be willing to sacrifice the hope, the peace, the friends, the insight that make his life what it is, to sacrifice them all for the sake of intimacy.

The hope he has had, if he has cared more for his relationship to the things of life than for the things themselves, will have been more a hope of being than of having. He will have hoped to be a man of spirit, to live the life of the spirit. The man of flesh in him will rouse him to a hope of having, a hope of intimacy, of sharing the life of another. As that hope awakens, he feels more and more acutely his lack of intimacy, and the lack of it drives him contrariwise toward a despair of it, toward a growing conviction that there is no hope of intimacy in his life. When intimacy does come then into his life, it comes as a great surprise, as the fulfillment of a hope he hardly dared to entertain. With the fulfillment of his new hope, he finds himself beginning to hope more intensely and to fear losing the person who has entered his life and shared life with him. The inner peace he enjoyed when his heart was set only on being begins to slip away from him. He begins to be involved more and more in the ins and outs of having and not having. The kind of friendship he once enjoyed, friendship without intimacy, begins to seem insufficient, and he begins to live more and more out of intimate relations. Insight that came easily when he was at peace will be hard to come by. He will have to fight his way through the growing chaos of his life to gain it.

A crisis will begin to develop in his life, a crisis in the root sense of the Greek word *krisis*, a "separation," here a separation of flesh and spirit. It will seem to him that he is beginning to lead a double life. Previously he gave his heart to the life of the spirit. Now his heart is divided between the life of the spirit and the life of the flesh. He still wants the hope, the peace, the friends, the insight that go with the life of the spirit, but he wants also to enjoy intimacy, to be caught up in the things of life. His life has become complex. When he is with the person he loves, he wonders whether his heart is fully in the things he is doing, the loving and sharing and tenderness. When he is with his friends, he finds himself distracted, unable to muster the enthusiasm he once had in their company, estranging them by his half-heartedness. When he is alone, he feels the passion again for the life of the spirit, but he is uneasy about it, wondering whether some insight will come that will unify his life again, wondering whether his heart will eventually become whole and undivided.

He longs for simplicity. He wants a simple life but wants its simplicity to encompass the richness of the flesh as well as the spirit. He can almost envision the life he wants. It would be a life of being rather than having, but the being would be richer than before. To be a man of flesh as well as a man of spirit, to be a whole man, that would be his hope. To let himself be caught up in the things of life, to go knowingly and willingly through the ins and outs of their seasons, that would be his peace. Then he could bring a whole heart to friendship, a heart of flesh as well as spirit. Then too he could live by insight, a richer insight than before, an insight that penetrates not only the spirit but also the flesh. He can almost envision it, but not quite. He does not yet possess that richer insight. He does not possess it because he appears not yet to have the basis for it, the richer being, the wholeness that he desires. How is he to find his way to wholeness without insight? And yet how is he to gain insight without becoming whole? He has come up against the unknown.

All he can do, it seems, is wait for insight to come, wait for wholeness to come. He cannot achieve insight without wholeness nor wholeness without insight. So it seems he cannot really achieve them at all. He can only wait for them, wait for them to come, wait for them to be given to him. Thus the crisis, the separation of flesh and spirit in his life, can lead to a withdrawal in which he waits for flesh and spirit to come together. The essence of the withdrawal is a waiting, a staying in readiness and expectation. Let us say that he does withdraw somehow and wait. Not being whole and undivided, not possessing already the insight that goes with wholeness, he does not fully know what he is waiting for or what is awaiting him. "He would again be as solitary as ever," Dostoevsky says of Ivan, "and though he had great hopes, and great—too great—expectations from life, he could not have given any definite account of his hopes, his expectations, or even his desires."[8]

Like Ivan, the man we are imagining is "as solitary as ever." He was already rather solitary before when he was trying to live without intimacy. Now that intimacy has come into his life and the man of flesh has risen up within him, he is still solitary in that he has not the wholeness to be wholly in any relationship with another. He is with himself more fully, though, and has withdrawn into himself, in that both parts of him, the man of spirit and the man of flesh, are present to him now, and he finds himself trying to come to grips with himself in his solitude. His "great—too great—expectations from life" make him dissatisfied with his life as it has been, a life of spirit without flesh, and also as it is, a life of spirit and flesh disjointed from one another. Whether a man wants an untrammeled life of the flesh or an untrammeled life of the spirit or an integral life of flesh and spirit, his expectations are "great—too great." For he finds himself living a life in which there is both flesh and spirit, each hampering and trammeling the other.

His "great—too great—expectations from life" can lead him in fact to hate the life and the world he knows. For the only life he knows, the only world he knows, is one in which flesh and spirit are divided against one another. His No, like Ivan's, may stop at the world and not reach all the way to God: "It's not that I don't accept God, you must understand, it's the world created by him I don't and cannot accept." The man we are envisioning has reason to stop short of God since he has already experienced a considerable change in the life and the world he knows, from a life without intimacy to a double life of flesh and spirit. If such a change is possible, then maybe a further change is possible to a life in which flesh and spirit are in harmony. Maybe there is an unknown within the life and the world he knows, an unknown man within him and an unknown God who can bring that man forth into being. Ivan, it is true, may have been saying "It's not that I don't accept God" merely for the sake of argument with Alyosha. The man we are envisioning, however, could say it without equivocation.

Instead of saying "It's the world created by him I don't and cannot accept," he would have to say "It's the world I know which I don't and cannot accept." To say "it's the world created by him" would mean there is nothing more to hope for from God. Yet he hopes for much more, waiting as he does for wholeness and insight. His relationship to the unknown, to the unknown man within him and to the unknown God, is more fundamental to him than his relationship to the world he knows. If it were the other way around, if his relationship to the known world were more fundamental, then his solitude would be final and his hatred of the world would be pure. He would live in the "bell jar" that Sylvia Plath describes when she says "to the person in the bell jar, blank and stopped as a dead baby, the world itself is the bad dream." All he could do would be perhaps to narrate that bad dream, as she did in her novel and in the poems written on the eve of her suicide.[9] As it is, his hatred is composed of love, love of flesh and love of spirit, and it is overborne by hope, the hope that is implicit in his waiting.

He does not set a definite limit to his waiting, let us say, as Ivan does. Ivan tells Alyosha that he will wait until he is thirty and then commit suicide.[10] A definite limit might make sense if a man were waiting only on the world he knows. It doesn't seem to make sense, though, if he is waiting on the unknown. If he were waiting on the world he knows, he would be waiting on the things of life and their seasons. There would be a season for the thing he awaits and a time when the season would be past. Ivan, for example, is waiting until thirty, until the end of youth, that is, with the idea that there is hope only so long as he is still young. To wait for flesh and spirit to come together, though, is to wait on something that has to do with all things and all seasons. It is not something that has to come in youth. It can come in manhood, in old age, perhaps even in death. It is a man within the man, a whole man of flesh and spirit, a new man hidden in the child, the youth, the man, and the old man.

Waiting on the unknown amounts to waiting on this man within the man, it seems, waiting on him to come forth and waiting on God to bring him forth. Waiting is like praying, and insight, when it comes, is like the answer to prayer. Are all insights glimpses of the new man, the whole man of flesh and spirit? If it is true that he is already there hidden in the child, the youth, the man, and the old man, then it may be possible to have glimpses of him at every age. But maybe insights are not so much glimpses of the whole man as his glimpses, not so much insights into him as his insights. When an insight occurs, a man goes beyond the world he knows into the realm of the unknown. Like Archimedes he can move the world he knows if he is given a place to stand outside it. The place to stand, it seems, is the unknown. Taking his stand on the unknown within him, he can see beyond the world he knows. Taking his stand on wholeness, he can see beyond the split world of flesh and spirit.

The world he knows changes with every insight. For the man we have been envisioning, it was first a world where flesh prevailed, where the things of life would enter into his life whether he liked it or not. Then it became a world where spirit prevailed, where he attained a steadfast relationship to the things of life that could carry through all their ins and outs. Now it has become a world where spirit and flesh exist side by side but not yet in harmony, where intimacy has entered into his life and involved him once again in the ins and outs of the things of life. Each time his world has been moved, it seems, there has been a place for him to stand outside it. If there had been nothing in his life more powerful than flesh, he would never have gotten beyond the point where the things of life entered his life whether he liked it or not. And if there had been nothing more powerful than spirit, he would never have gotten beyond his steadfast relationship to the things of life carrying through their ins and outs with a serenity like that of the archaic smile.

Now, as he waits for flesh and spirit to come together, he

is waiting on whatever it is that is more powerful than either flesh or spirit. He is waiting on the whole man who has come forth somehow at every juncture of his life. He is waiting for him to come forth now, not only to see but also to be seen, not only to understand but to be understood, not only to have insight but to be penetrated by insight. As he recalls the junctures of his life and the insights he has had, he begins to realize that the whole man is already emerging while he is waiting. The waiting is itself the beginning. Who is it who is waiting on the new man? Is it the man of flesh or the man of spirit? Is it the divided man of spirit and flesh? Or is it not the new man himself, waiting to come forth?

It begins to appear that the man who is dissatisfied with the split world, the one who waits on the unknown man within him to come forth, is himself the new man. He is himself the whole man of flesh and spirit, and he has been there all along. His waiting on the new man is a waiting on himself; it is the new man's waiting to come forth. His coming then is a "realization" in the double sense of that word, a coming to know and a coming to be. He has been there all along in the child, the youth, the man, but he does not come forth until he knows, until he realizes that he has been there all along. He is the one who suffers the crisis, the separation of his flesh and his spirit, and he is the one who withdraws and waits. It is as though he has come to the place appointed for meeting the new man. It is a solitary place. He has come and is waiting. No one else comes. Then he begins to realize that no one else will come, that the new man has already come to meet him, that he himself is the new man.

If he is the new man, the whole man of flesh and spirit, where is his wholeness? Where is the richer being that he

has been awaiting? There should be some point within him
where the split between flesh and spirit ceases. "Everything
which belongs to an individual's life shall enter into it," Jung
says, "whether he consents or not, or is conscious of what is
happening to him or not."[11] That is the split between flesh
and spirit. On the one side there is flesh, the things of life entering his life and passing from it. On the other side there is
spirit, his consciousness or unconsciousness, his willingness
or unwillingness. As the things of life enter and pass, nevertheless, it does make a difference whether he consents or not.
It does make a difference whether he is conscious of what is
happening to him or not. That must be the point where the
split between flesh and spirit ceases. What difference does
it make? That is the question that must be answered by the
self-realization of the whole man. He is present all along because it makes a difference. He comes forth at last when he
realizes what difference it makes.

The difference seems to be a matter of power. When a
man is unconscious, or when he is conscious of what is happening to him but does not consent to it, he appears to be the
prey and also the instrument of powers that are inhuman.
A creative power seems to be at work in his life causing the
things of life to enter into it, and a destructive power seems
to be at work causing them to pass from it once again. What
is more, the creative and destructive powers seem to work
through his life upon other lives. When he becomes conscious where he was unconscious and willing where he was
unwilling, however, the powers seem to disappear. He seems
to become simply human. The things of life enter his life
and pass from it, conscious and willing as he is, without any
show of power. He seems to have given up any power he

might have had over others, and at the same time freed himself from any power that might have dominated him. He walks away starkly simple and free, starkly human. Yet there is a kind of power in that too, the power of the whole man, the power that is more powerful than either flesh or spirit.

That power, the power of the new man within him, appears to be in fact the power of God at work within him, for it does what the power of a creator would do. It draws him through phases of becoming, from nothingness into being. When he becomes aware of that power, when he sees how it has been at work in his life all along, then he can begin to live in touch with it. As he gives himself over to that power, the other powers that had dominated his life, the creative and destructive powers of the flesh, the controlling power of the spirit, all seem to wane and to lose their role in his life. The whole man thus is not a balance of opposing powers, the creative and destructive powers of the flesh balanced against one another and balanced together against the controlling power of the spirit. He is led by another power altogether, a power that has its own goal and its own way, a power that leads him out of his withdrawal and solitude into an entirely new adventure.

## 2. *The Withdrawal and the Return*

The new adventure is a return among men. When a man has been solitary he may long for companionship, just as one who has been living constantly and inescapably with others may long for solitude. There is a deep solitude, though, that no human companionship seems able to take away. One may discover it when an intimate relationship seems to fail, when

one has expected the intimate person to make one unalone
and one finds oneself still alone. The man we have been
envisioning, who has suffered a crisis of flesh and spirit, finds
that deep solitude in all his relationships with others. He is
so divided that he cannot be wholly in any relationship, it
seems to him, except at certain moments, like moments of
insight, when the whole man in him comes forth, moments
when he shares the enthusiasm of an insight with others.
These are moments of giving when he seems to touch the
whole being of another, and moments of receiving when another seems to touch his whole being.

"When you direct your mind to purity and straightfor-
wardness even for one moment," Hui Neng says, "you are a
Buddha."[12] When the whole man comes forth even for a moment, perhaps we could say, a man is a sage or a prophet. For
in that moment his whole being is touched or he touches the
whole being of another. He is a sage or a prophet for that moment. The life of a sage or a prophet is in fact a life of withdrawal and return.[13] He withdraws into solitude to attain
insight and then returns to share his insight with other
men.[14] Gotama withdrew into the forest for seven years and
then returned to spend the remaining years of his life sharing
his enlightenment with others. Jesus withdrew into the desert
for forty days and then returned to spend his short public life
sharing the revelation he had received. The man we have
been envisioning goes through a withdrawal and a return too.
He goes through a crisis of flesh and spirit and then withdraws to find wholeness. Now he is about to return to share
whatever insight he has with others. Is he then a sage or a
prophet? Only at moments when the whole man comes forth,
only when his whole being is touched or he touches that of

another. Every man, it seems, is a sage or a prophet in such
moments.

There are especially two such moments in the story of the
Karamazovs. One is when Alyosha kisses Ivan; the other is
when Alyosha kisses the earth. Each is the moment of a kiss,
a moment of touching and being touched. When he kisses
Ivan, he is kissing the man who withdraws from the world;
the man who returns is kissing the man who withdraws. He
is saying Yes to the man who says No to the world; he is loving the man who hates the world. When he kisses the earth,
on the other hand, he is kissing the world itself. He is returning to the world, saying Yes to the world, loving the world.
He touches and is touched in both moments. All through
the story he is touched whenever he touches another and he
touches whenever he is touched by another. He is usually
listening rather than speaking. He listens to his brothers,
to Dimitri, to Ivan. He listens to the three women who correspond to the three brothers, to Grushenka, to Katya, to
Lise. He listens to the sage Zossima. He listens to the child
Kolya. All the most important things each person in the story
has to say are said to him. He is touched by each in turn,
and yet he touches each of them, somehow calling forth
whatever is in their minds and hearts.

Instead of a sage or a prophet who speaks to men like
Gotama or Jesus, therefore, let us imagine a man who returns
like Alyosha to listen, to speak and to listen, but especially to
listen. The man we have been imagining, divided as he is
between flesh and spirit and whole only in moments when
he touches and is touched, might do well to listen more than
speak, though he could speak too out of those moments of
wholeness and insight. Say he listens like Alyosha and

touches as he is touched. Say he listens first to the man within him who withdraws like Ivan, the man who is solitary in spite of all relationships. Say he listens then to the earth, to everything from which the solitary man is withdrawn.

He may find it easier to hear what the man within him is saying, the man who is solitary like Ivan, if he listens to another person who is solitary and who is not afraid to put aloneness into words. Another person may say things to him that he has not dared to say to himself. A woman, for example, may say to him in effect, "We are alone, you and I, and we cannot make one another unalone." She speaks of the deep solitude that no human companionship can seem to take away. He has not dared to admit to himself, let us say, that there is such a solitude but has lived in the hope that intimacy with another would make him unalone. To say "we are alone," to be sure, is to utter a paradox. It can mean not only "you are alone and I am alone" but also "we are together in our aloneness." There is a compassion toward one another, a being with one another in aloneness, that becomes possible once it is recognized that "we cannot make one another unalone."

As long as he hopes to become unalone through intimacy, a man cannot have that compassion, cannot be with another in that way, particularly not with the person with whom he seeks to be intimate. Instead he is always expecting the other to make him unalone, to take away his solitude, and he is always being disappointed. His feelings toward the other become a mixture of hope and disappointment. He begins to bear in his heart not only love but also a grudge. His feelings toward himself are mixed too. Originally he had hardly hoped for intimacy with another person, let us suppose, and his solitude had been a kind of quiet despair. Now he finds that intimacy is possible for him, and yet he finds himself still somehow alone in the midst of it. His despair has become unquiet. His desire to become unalone is an unwillingness to be with himself. To give up now the hope of being unalone would be quite a different thing from giving up, as he once did, the hope of intimacy. It would mean becoming willing to be with himself and becoming able, because of that willingness, to be with another in aloneness.

To say "we are alone, and we cannot make one another unalone" is to say that we live in a wilderness, a world of solitude, that our world is like a desert or a forest. Allah, in the Koran, calls man "him whom I created lonely."[15] If that were the human situation and a man were unwilling to be alone, he would find himself always at odds with the world. He would not be like a man who had deliberately withdrawn into a desert or a forest to seek solitude but rather like one who was lost in a wilderness, who was left to himself against his will. We have been envisioning a man somewhat like that, alone and unwilling to be alone. As he listens now to another who is alone, he realizes it, he realizes both his aloneness and his unwillingness. Suppose he finds also that there are times when he is willing to be alone. Sometimes he is happy in his aloneness, like a child playing alone or like a man dwelling in the wilderness. At other times he is unhappy with it, like a lost child or like a man wandering in the wilderness and unable to find a path that leads out of it. He is happy and unhappy in the wilderness, willing and unwilling to be alone.

What makes a man happy when he is alone and happy? What makes a child happy when he is playing alone? There may be a clue in the word "alone." The word is a combination of the two words "all" and "one." There was probably no deep wisdom in putting them together: to say someone was "all one" probably meant no more than we mean when we say someone is "all alone." The combination can lead one who thinks about it, nevertheless, to what may be an insight, that to be alone is to be all one. When a man is with himself, that is, he may be whole. When the child is playing alone, when the man is alone and happy, he may be all one. He may feel his body from within as he feels his mind. He may be in touch with his flesh and his spirit. He may be in touch with the unknown dwelling within him, the unknown God at work in his life and the unknown man that the God is bringing forth, the unknown man that he is when he is all one.

What then makes him unhappy when he is alone and unhappy? There are words for unhappiness derived from "alone" such as "lone" and "lonely" and "lonesome." They suggest a lack of companionship combined with a longing for it and a feeling of dreariness. Where do the lack and the longing and the dreariness come from? When he is alone, when he is without another, a man is one, someone, everyone, anyone, no one. He is, as Sartre describes himself in the last sentence of his autobiography, "a whole man, composed of all men and as good as all of them and no better than any."[16] He is everything that man is, and yet he cannot wholly use or enjoy any of it by himself. He is everything that man is—that must be what gives him his sense of well-being when he is alone and happy. Yet he cannot wholly use or enjoy any of it by himself—that must be what gives him his sense of lack and longing and dreariness when he is alone and unhappy. His life is like Greek drama in its early days when there was only one actor and a chorus. He is the one actor and mankind is the chorus. To make things otherwise he has to do something parallel to what Aeschylus did when he brought in a second actor.[17]

It is the one actor standing before the chorus of mankind who can say he is "a whole man, composed of all men and as good as all of them and no better than any." What his life lacks are the two elements that came into drama when the second actor was introduced, conversation and interaction between one person and another. Conversation begins when he begins to listen and to hear the voice of another person above the contending voices within him. Insofar as he is still divided within himself, there are many voices already within him—the voice of his flesh, the voice of his spirit, the voice of the whole man—and it is difficult to hear above them the voice of another person. When he does begin to listen, he can hear at first only what the solitary man within him echoes. A woman enters, we have imagined. She is the second actor. She says to him in effect, "We are alone, you and I, and we cannot make one another unalone." He listens to her, for the solitary man within him echoes what she says. It is as though he were saying it himself, and to that extent it is as though there were still only one actor.

Interaction begins when he does something in response to what is said to him. There is apparently nothing more to be said. Or before any more can be said, there is something to be done. Alyosha kisses Ivan, the solitary man, after listening to him. Suppose then the man we are envisioning kisses the woman and in kissing he touches the solitary woman in her and she touches the solitary man in him.

The kiss does not refute what she is saying. It does not say, "We are not alone, you and I, and we can indeed make one another unalone." Alyosha's kiss similarly does not refute what Ivan is saying. Ivan has been telling a story he has composed about Jesus coming back among men and meeting a grand inquisitor. The inquisitor says to Jesus in effect (as Dostoevsky puts it briefly in his notebooks), "I love humanity more than you do."[18] Jesus says nothing in reply but kisses the inquisitor. Alyosha, hearing the story, then kisses Ivan.[19]

"I love humanity more than you do," the inquisitor is saying to Jesus and Ivan is saying to Alyosha, "for you would give man to himself but I would take away man's burden." Jesus then kisses the inquisitor and Alyosha kisses Ivan for loving humanity as he does. The woman we have been envisioning is saying "We cannot take away one another's aloneness." The man who listens then kisses her for loving him as she does. Her love is the reverse of the inquisitor's and Ivan's, for she would give a man to himself and not try to take away his burden. Kissing her, a man receives himself from her and she receives herself from him. She gives him to himself and he gives her to herself. Each one becomes whole in that moment of giving and receiving, each one becomes "all one," and yet each one receives that wholeness, that all-oneness, from the other, each one gives it to the other. A man's all-oneness cannot be taken away, it seems, and yet it can be given and received, and when it is given and received, his life ceases to be a drama like Ivan's or the inquisitor's in which there is only one actor and the chorus of humanity and becomes instead a drama of human intercourse.

Imagine now a life in which giving and receiving have just

begun, a life in which a second person has just entered. It is like the historic moment when the second actor was introduced by Aeschylus into Greek drama. "With the second actor came the dialogue and the indefinite possibilities of the reaction of some characters on others," Borges says. "A prophetic spectator would have seen that multitudes of future appearances accompanied him: Hamlet and Faust and Segismundo and Macbeth and Peer Gynt and others our eyes cannot yet discern."[20] The moment when a second person enters seems equally consequential in a life. It is a turning point, a moment of enlightenment and revelation. Indefinite possibilities appear. With the woman who has entered the life of the man we have been imagining there come indefinite possibilities of receiving from her what he is—and he is everything that a human being is—and of giving her what she is—and she too is everything that a human being is.

A multitude of future appearances accompany her. Once his life has been opened through her to human intercourse, many other persons can enter it. Say he realizes that he is "all one." Say he realizes that his all-oneness cannot be taken away from him by another. Say he realizes also that it can be given and received. Say he begins therefore to listen like Alyosha, to receive what he is from others and to give others what they are. Not everyone, it is true, gives him everything that he is. He finds himself talking and acting differently with different persons. Some evoke in him the man of spirit; others evoke the man of flesh; others evoke the whole man. With some he is a Hamlet, a divided man who is always questioning himself; with others he is a Faust, a man of spirit who is striving to become incarnate; with others he is a Segismundo, a man who is striving to escape the bondage

of the flesh and live the life of the spirit; with others he is a
Macbeth, a man who is fascinated with the destructive power
of the flesh; with others he is a Peer Gynt, a man who is
fascinated with the creative power of the flesh.

When he listens to the voice of spirit in another, he becomes a man of spirit. When he listens to the voice of flesh,
he becomes a man of flesh. It is only when he listens to the
whole human being, as it seems, that he becomes "all one."
What is it then to listen to the whole human being? "We can
know more than we can tell," Polanyi says, "and we can tell
nothing without relying on our awareness of things we may
not be able to tell."[21] When a person tells of the flesh, of the
things of his life, he is relying on the spirit, on his relationship to the things. When he tells of the spirit, on the other
hand, of his relationship to the things, he is relying on the
flesh, on the things of his life and their times. To hear the
whole human being one must listen not only to what he is
telling but also to what he is relying on and may be unable to
tell. Consider again the words "We are alone, you and I, and
we cannot make one another unalone." They tell of the flesh,
of intimacy, the limits of intimacy. They rely, though, on the
spirit, on a consciousness of what it is to be together and what
it is to be alone, on a willingness to be together and a willingness to be alone.

To hear only what the other person is telling of in saying
"We are alone" is to hear only of the failure and the limits of
intimacy. It is to receive a rebuff. The man of flesh is evoked
only to be frustrated. To hear also what the other person is relying on in telling of aloneness, though, is to hear of the consciousness and especially of the willingness of the other. It is
to hear the whole human being. It is to receive the love of the

other, a love that gives the whole man to himself. The words "We can know more than we can tell, and we can tell nothing without relying on our awareness of things we may not be able to tell" somehow respond and correspond to the words "We are alone, you and I, and we cannot make one another unalone." We are alone, it seems, because we can know more than we can tell. If we could tell everything, we could become unalone. Because we are alone, because we cannot make one another unalone, there is "a time to embrace and a time to refrain from embracing."[22] Because we can know more than we can tell, because we cannot tell everything, there is "a time to keep silence and a time to speak."[23] Still, we can listen to one another, not only to the things we can tell but also to each other's awareness of things we may not be able to tell.

Listening to the tacit element in what we are saying to one another, giving heed to the awareness of things we may not be able to tell, is like listening to the earth. It amounts to giving heed to the human situation out of which we are speaking, giving heed to the world of flesh in which we are dwelling as we speak of the spirit, giving heed to the world of spirit in which we are dwelling as we speak of the flesh. Just before Ahab said, "Let me look into a human eye; it is better than to gaze into sea or sky, better than to gaze upon God," Starbuck saw him, "and he seemed to hear in his own true heart the measureless sobbing that stole out of the centre of the serenity all around."[24] Listening to that measureless sobbing, he was listening to the world in which Ahab was dwelling when he said, "Let me look into a human eye." It is like listening to the world in which a person is dwelling who says, "We are alone." The world one hears is a world of aloneness and all-oneness, a world of "measureless sobbing" and "serenity all around."

The world that drives one to exclaim "Let me look into a human eye" is a world with aloneness at its heart; the "measureless sobbing" comes "out of the centre of the serenity all around." The world that gives one the courage to say "We are alone," on the other hand, is a world with all-oneness at its heart; the serenity comes "out of the centre" of the "measureless sobbing." The one world calls forth a No like Ivan's; the other calls forth a Yes like Alyosha's. The man we have been envisioning has encountered both worlds. Listening now to the worlds in which other persons dwell, he begins to wonder, let us say, which is the true one. What is at the center of the world? Is it aloneness and measureless sobbing? Or is it all-oneness and serenity? Listening, however, even to the world with aloneness at its heart, gives him a sense of all-oneness. The world of solitude, as he listens to the whole human being who dwells in it, becomes an integral world of flesh and spirit. However divided a person is, if one listens not only to what he is saying but also to what he is relying on as he says it, one hears the whole human being. The listening itself, the giving of heed, is a giving of wholeness.

Thus Alyosha is able to kiss both Ivan and the earth. When he kisses the earth, he rises up a new man. "It was as though some idea had seized the sovereignty of his mind—and it was for all his life and for ever and ever," Dostoevsky says. "He had fallen on the earth a weak boy, but he rose up a resolute champion and he knew and felt it suddenly at the very moment of his ecstasy."[25] There is an image of wholeness here, but the wholeness is not in the earth by itself. It is rather in the man and the earth together, the man kissing the

earth. Let us imagine a man kissing the earth. Let it be the
man we have been envisioning. The earth here is the world
of flesh, the world of the things of life and the times of life.
The kissing of the earth is the relationship a man has to the
earth, to the things and times of life, when he is whole. The
idea that seizes the sovereignty of his mind and makes him do
it is not an idea of the goodness of the earth by itself so much
as an idea of the wholeness of the man who kisses the earth.
By itself the earth—the world of flesh, the world of intimacy
and of the limits and failure of intimacy—is a world of aloneness. It is the man kissing the earth, the man and the earth
together in the kissing, that is the world of all-oneness.

The world of aloneness is a hell; the world of all-oneness is
a heaven. The earth is a hell for a man when he holds apart
from it, a heaven when he kisses it. When he holds apart
from the earth, his No to the world is somehow in agreement
with the God who said, "It is not good for man to be alone."[26]
When he kisses the earth, his Yes to the world is somehow in
agreement with the God who "saw everything that he had
made and, behold, it was very good."[27] Somehow he is with
God and God is with him both in his aloneness and in his all-
oneness. When Ahab says "Let me look into a human eye,"
he adds "it is better than to gaze into sea or sky, better than to
gaze upon God." In the world of aloneness where he has
been dwelling, he has been with God, gazing into sea and
sky, gazing upon God. It is the God, nevertheless, the creating power at work in a man's life, that drives him to seek human companionship, that makes him dissatisfied with the
world of aloneness, that makes him exclaim "Let me look into
a human eye." It is the creating power then, the God in his
life, that leads a man into the world of all-oneness, that leads

him to receive what he is from others and give others what they are, that finally seizes the sovereignty of his mind with the idea of kissing the earth.

We have been telling a story of man, the story of a man who goes through a crisis of flesh and spirit, then withdraws into solitude to come to grips with himself, and then returns among men to receive and to give wholeness. Implicit in the story of the man is a story of God. Perhaps that is always the way with stories of God and man. When we tell of man, we are relying on our awareness of things we may not be able to tell of God, and when we tell of God, we are relying on our awareness of things we may not be able to tell of man. The tacit element in a story of man is a story of God, while the tacit element in a story of God is a story of man. God is the unknown in a story of man, while man is the unknown in a story of God.

The man we have been telling of is a man of spirit in whom there arises a man of flesh. When the man of flesh rises up in him, a crisis occurs, a separation of flesh and spirit. Up to this point in his life, God has appeared to be in alliance with spirit. Now, as the man of flesh arises, God appears to be in alliance with flesh too, with the creative and even the destructive powers of the flesh. Or rather, God appears to be leading the man toward a wholeness that is greater than either flesh or spirit. Three faces of God appear. First there is the God of spirit. He appears to lead a man by insight, to lead him from one insight to another, to lead him into an existence where there is hope and peace and friends. Then there is the God of flesh. He appears to lead a man by dread and fascination rather than by insight, to lead him by the dread and fascination of sexuality and mortality, to lead him into an

existence where love and hatred, desire and disgust, joy and
sorrow, fear and daring, hope and despair have each their
time. Then there is the God of the whole man. He appears
to lead a man by what happens to him, for instance, by the
rising of the man of flesh within him, to lead him nevertheless by insight into what happens to him, to lead him into an
integral existence where what happens to him happens with
his consciousness and consent.

To gain insight into what is happening to him the man we
have been telling of withdraws into solitude. Actually he has
been living in solitude all along in that his lack of wholeness
has prevented him from being wholly in any relationship
with another person. Now, though, he begins to wait in solitude. His withdrawal is a waiting on insight, a waiting on the
whole man, a waiting on God. Insight comes when he realizes that in spite of his dividedness he is already the whole
man waiting to come forth and that God is already at work in
his life drawing him forth into being. He is already the whole
man and yet he has still to come forth. God is already at work
in his life and yet God has still to complete his work and rest
from it as he does on the seventh day of Genesis. Sensing that
he is already the whole man, that he is everything that a man
is, he feels alone and happy like a child playing alone. To be
alone is to be "all one." Sensing, on the other hand, that he
has still to come forth, that in spite of being everything that
a man is, he cannot seem to use or enjoy any of it by himself,
he feels alone and unhappy. He longs for human companionship. It is like the moment in Genesis when God says "It is
not good for man to be alone."

He returns therefore among men. He ceases to wait in solitude and goes among others to receive wholeness and to give

it in his turn. He finds, however, that there is a solitude he cannot escape. "We are alone," he is told, "and we cannot make one another unalone." There is a deep aloneness, he learns, that human companionship cannot seem to take away. As he learns this from another, as he receives his aloneness from another, he realizes that this aloneness, though it cannot be taken away, can nevertheless be given and received. And when it is given and received, he finds that it becomes an all-oneness, a wholeness. To receive his wholeness from another he finds that he must listen to the whole other, not only to what is said but also to what is unsaid and perhaps cannot be said. At the same time, giving heed to what is unsaid as well as to what is said, he gives a wholeness to the other. The world is changed for him from a world of aloneness to a world of all-oneness. He ends by kissing the earth. It is like the moment in Genesis when "God saw everything that he had made and, behold, it was very good."

There are three moments in our story: first there is a moment of crisis, a moment of dividedness; then there is a moment of withdrawal, a moment of aloneness; and then there is a moment of return, a moment of all-oneness. If we make no mention of God, if we leave the tacit element of our story completely tacit, then the story is very similar to that of Gotama's withdrawal and return. Gotama, "the silent sage," makes no mention of God, makes no attempt to speak of what God is (Brahman) or even of what man is (Atman).[28] The three moments, if we follow his example in leaving the tacit element tacit, appear to be three experiences of solitude. There is first the kind of solitude one experiences when one is with others but is so divided that one is unable to be wholly with them. Then there is the kind of solitude one experiences when one is by oneself, sometimes happy, sometimes unhappy to be with oneself. And then there is the transfigured solitude one experiences when one is with others and yet with oneself, able to give them what they are and receive from them what one is. When we begin to speak of what they are and what one is, however, we are beginning to speak of what man is and are not far from speaking of what God is.

If we do begin to speak of God, if we do not leave the tacit element of our story tacit, then the story begins to sound more like that of the withdrawal and return of Jesus. He of course does speak of God, even calls God by the familiar name "Abba." The three moments, if we follow his example in speaking of God, appear to be three decisive moments in a struggle with God much like the story of Jacob wrestling with God. There is first a moment when the struggle is going on within man, a struggle between flesh and spirit with God appearing to side now with man's spirit, now with man's flesh. Then there is a moment when the struggle changes into a head-on struggle between man and God, an apparent deadlock with man waiting on God and God waiting on man. And then there is a moment when the struggle with God appears to be over and there remains only a struggle of man with man. At that moment Jacob receives the new name "Israel," asks God his own name in turn, and gets the reply "Why do you ask my name?"[29] It is perhaps at that moment in his own life, the moment when the struggle with God in the wilderness is over, that Jesus begins to call God "Abba."[30]

Where our story differs from both that of Gotama and that of Jesus is in the listening that occurs on the return. Gotama and Jesus come back from the wilderness to speak, Gotama keeping silence about God, Jesus calling God "Abba." The man in our story, though, comes back from solitude to listen, to speak and to listen but especially to listen. When a man speaks out of his own insight, he remains one person, although he speaks to many. When a man listens to many persons, though, he is in danger of becoming many himself. He hears many names of God and seems to have many names himself, each person he listens to evoking in him a different person. To become "all one" he must listen to the whole human being who speaks to him. To gain his own unity he must give the other person a unity by listening not only to what he is saying but also to what he is leaving unsaid. He must listen not only to the express but also to the tacit element of the other person's story. He must hear the name of the other's God. His own struggle with God, therefore, does not cease when he returns among men and his life becomes a struggle of man with man.

He spends his life struggling with God. He is like the old man who spent his life struggling with the sea. "Everything about him was old except his eyes and they were the same color as the sea and were cheerful and undefeated." There is something about the man who struggles with God too that never grows old. It is perhaps the fact that he is "all one." His all-oneness is a sort of kinship with God, like having "eyes the same color as the sea." It always emerges in his struggles with God and makes him seem "cheerful and undefeated." Because of his kinship with God he can call God by a familiar name, as Jesus did, though he is always meeting God in strange and unfamiliar guises. Or he can keep silence about God as Gotama did, though God remains always the tacit element in his story. And whether he speaks of God or keeps silence, he is able to hear God, like hearing the sea, in the speech and in the silence of others.

# NOTES TO CHAPTER THREE

1. Ernest Hemingway, *The Old Man and the Sea* (New York, Scribner's, 1952), p. 10.
2. Fyodor Dostoevsky, *The Brothers Karamazov*, tr. by Constance Garnett (Chicago, Encyclopaedia Britannica, 1955), p. 317.
3. Ibid., p. 121.
4. Sylvia Plath, *The Bell Jar* (New York, Bantam Books, 1972), p. 193.
5. Dostoevsky, op. cit., p. 313.
6. Dostoevsky, *The Notebooks for the Brothers Karamazov*, ed. and tr. by Edward Wasiolek (Chicago, University of Chicago Press, 1971), p. 202.
7. Ecclesiastes 3:4ff.
8. Dostoevsky, *The Brothers Karamazov*, p. 137.
9. Cf. Sylvia Plath, *Ariel* (New York, Harper & Row, 1965). These were the poems written on the eve of her suicide in 1963. Cf. particularly the one called *The Hanging Man* (p. 69) where she says of God, "If he were I, he would do what I did."
10. Dostoevsky, *The Brothers Karamazov*, pp. 118f., 137. Cf. *The Notebooks for the Brothers Karamazov*, p. 73, where the idea of suicide is more explicit.
11. C. G. Jung, *Answer to Job*, tr. by R. F. C. Hull (New York, Meridian, 1960), p. 184.
12. *The Sutra of Hui Neng*, p. 109, in *The Diamond Sutra and the Sutra of Hui Neng*, tr. by A. F. Price and Wong Mou-lam (Berkeley, Shambala, 1969).
13. Cf. Arnold Toynbee, *A Study of History*, Vol. 3 (London, Oxford University Press, 1934), pp. 248ff., on the pattern of withdrawal and return in the lives of the creative personalities of history.
14. Cf. my book *The Way of All the Earth* (New York, Macmillan, 1972), pp. xff., 14ff., 38ff., 147ff., 165ff., 221ff., on the pattern of withdrawal and return in the great religions and especially in the lives of Gotama and Jesus.

15. Sura LXXIV, 11. Mohammed M. Pickthall, *The Meaning of the Glorious Koran* (New York, New American Library, 1953), has "him whom I created lonely"; Arthur J. Arberry, *The Koran Interpreted* (New York, Macmillan, 1970), has "him whom I created alone"; Abdullah Yusuf Ali, *The Holy Qu-ran* (New York, Hafner, 1946), has "the [creature] whom I created [bare and] alone."

16. Jean-Paul Sartre, *The Words*, tr. by Bernard Frechtman (New York, Fawcett, 1966), p. 160.

17. Aristotle has it, in his *Poetics*, 1449a16, that Aeschylus introduced a second actor, reduced the role of the chorus, and made the dialogue the main business of the drama. One can see in Aeschylus' earlier plays (*Suppliant Maidens, Persians, Prometheus, Seven Against Thebes*) that the second actor tends at first to be only a messenger or a herald, a bearer of tidings, while in the *Oresteia* (*Agamemnon, Libation Bearers, Eumenides*) he tends to become another principal character in the story.

18. Dostoevsky, *The Notebooks for the Brothers Karamazov*, p. 75.

19. Dostoevsky, *The Brothers Karamazov*, pp. 136 (Jesus kisses the inquisitor) and 137 (Alyosha kisses Ivan).

20. Jorge Luis Borges, *Other Inquisitions*, tr. by Ruth L. C. Simms (New York, Washington Square Press, 1966), p. 177.

21. Michael Polanyi, *Personal Knowledge* (New York, Harper Torchbooks, 1964), p. x; this is Polanyi's statement of the thesis of his book. Cf. also his smaller book, *The Tacit Dimension* (Garden City, N.Y., Doubleday, 1966).

22. Ecclesiastes 3:5.

23. Ibid., 3:7.

24. Herman Melville, *Moby Dick*, ed. by Luther S. Mansfield and Howard P. Vincent (New York, Hendricks House, 1952), Chap. 132, p. 534.

25. Dostoevsky, *The Brothers Karamazov*, p. 191.

26. Genesis 2:18.

27. Genesis 1:31.

28. Cf. my book *The Way of All the Earth,* pp. 193, 219, on Atman as meaning "what man is" and Brahman as meaning "what God is" in the Upanishads. Cf. ibid., pp. 30, 231, on Gotama's silence on the subject of Atman and Brahman.
29. Genesis 32:29.
30. Cf. my book *A Search for God in Time and Memory* (New York, Macmillan, 1970), pp. x, 11, 113, 192ff., 222, on Jesus calling God "Abba."

# Conclusion

Ariel sings of the marvelous change that comes over a man's flesh when he drowns in the sea, how his bones become coral and his eyes become pearls:

> Nothing of him that doth fade,
> But doth suffer a sea-change
> Into something rich and strange.[1]

The things of a man's life, we have been saying, undergo some such change as this on account of his relationship to them. The things of his life enter his life and pass from it. They are the part of him "that doth fade." His relationship to them, his relationship to his love and hatred, his desire and disgust, his joy and sorrow, his fear and daring, his hope and despair, causes them all to "suffer a sea-change into something rich and strange."

A "sea-change" begins to take place when his life opens up before him all the way to death, when he becomes fully aware that death is in store for him, when he sees his course ahead with a kind of deadly clarity. Then he may flee from death and from the course that he has been following in life, the path that he sees leading to death. His flight from death and from the deadly clear path is already a relationship to his death and to the things of his life. It can become a quest of life like that of Gilgamesh, leading him out of the situation he is accustomed to and into a rich and strange wonderland. He may wander like Gilgamesh, always searching for a path that does not lead to death. Like Gilgamesh too he may fail. He may be unable to find a path that he can walk other than the one from which he has been fleeing. Or he may find other paths but find that each of them leads also to death, that each one, as soon as he sets foot on it, becomes a deadly clear path.

If he becomes convinced that every path leads to death, that there is no better way than the one he originally abandoned, he may set out to find his old way once again. Going back is a new quest and a new relationship to death and to the things of his life. It can be a journey home like that of Odysseus, leading him again through a wonderland and back to his homeland and his familiar path. When he comes back again to the familiar things of his life, he finds that they have all suffered "a sea-change into something rich and strange." Hope is not the same for him, now that he has tasted the hope of finding a path that does not lead to death and has been compelled by his experience to despair of ever finding it. Fear is not the same either, now that he has faced his fear of death and has found the courage to walk the deadly clear path. He has become "something rich and strange" himself, something hard and bright:

> Of his bones are coral made;
> Those are pearls that were his eyes . . .[2]

There is something strange about death and that strangeness enters his consciousness when death enters it. There is something rich too, like bones that have become coral or eyes that have become pearls. When he realizes the change that has come over him through his relationship to death, when he realizes how rich and strange he has become, he becomes capable of a new journey. Seeing how he can change, how the things of his life can change for him, he can be inspired to set out on a journey that has such change for its object. He can be caught up in a quest like Dante's, leading him out of the hell where he lives without hope and fear through a purgatory of renewed hope and fear to a paradise where he is moved by love. He goes not from path to path on this journey but from relationship to relationship. His path changes, ceases to be a deadly clear path, because his relationship to it changes, because he lets himself be moved by "the love that moves the sun and the other stars."

Seeing how he can be changed by love into "something rich and strange," richer and stranger than before, he may begin to desire all richness and strangeness, to desire all possible changes, and to fear missing any of the richness and strangeness that might come to him through change. That can set him upon an adventure like that of the Odysseus of Nikos Kazantzakis, leading him to explore all the possibilities of the human spirit, to roam the world of the human spirit from pole to pole. Here he meets a dilemma. If he seeks only to have the experience of all the possibilities, only to go through all the metamorphoses of which the human spirit is capable, then his adventure becomes its own goal. It leads nowhere outside itself but to death. Like the Odysseus of Kazantzakis he journeys toward death and death becomes his companion on the way. His path becomes once again a deadly clear path leading to death.

If he seeks, rather, to discover what the possibilities of the human spirit are, to be led by his discoveries, to let his discoveries determine his goals, he journeys into the unknown and the unknown becomes his companion. It is like letting himself be moved by "the love that moves the sun and the other stars." Discovery is only his provisional goal. His ultimate goal is unknown, for he seeks to be led wherever discovery will lead him. Now his path has lost its deadly clarity; it is no longer a clear path leading simply to death. It has become a path into the unknown. He must find his way discovery by discovery, insight by insight. Each insight illumines the way ahead. Each change he undergoes gives him some sense of where he is going.

Thinking back, he can see the unknown at work in his life story from the beginning. He can see how he has been led at each stage by the dread and the fascination of the unknown. As a child, he may have felt the dread of the unknown each time he had to enter into an unfamiliar world, when changing from one school to another, for example, or when first going from home to school, and no doubt when first coming from the womb into the world. He may have felt the fascination of the unknown, its power to draw, to compel, to captivate, whenever a world would become largely familiar like the world of home. There may have been enough strangeness to fascinate, to fill the world with gods, when there was no longer enough to terrify, to fill the world with demons. When sexuality began to rise and grow powerful in him at the age of puberty, however, the dread of sexuality and of the unknown in it may have tended to keep him away from intimacy, while the fascination of it and of the unknown in it may have so absorbed him that he did not learn to love. And now that the sense of mortality is rising in him with the passing of youth, the dread of death and of the unknown in it, he sees, can keep him from enjoying the time of his life, while the fascination of it and of the unknown in it can so absorb him that he does not learn to live.

To be led by the dread and the fascination of the unknown, he sees, is to be led without one's consent and without being conscious of what is happening to one. To be led by the unknown consciously and willingly, on the other hand, is to be led by insight rather than by the power of dread and fascination. Yet how is he to reach consciousness and consent? How is he to get beyond dread and fascination? Each thing that comes into his life—first the world, then sex, then death—appears to him dreadful and fascinating as long as he gazes upon it directly with his own eyes. If he looks into a human eye, though, into the eye of another person or even into his own eye as a child or a youth, thinking back on his life, he sees the dreadful and the fascinating reduced there to tiny human dimensions. It becomes like the tiny image of himself he sees when he looks into the pupil of another's eye. It loses its inhuman richness and strangeness and becomes something human.

"If you now beheld them, your affections would become tender," Ariel says to Prospero, speaking of his captives. "Dost thou think so, spirit?" Prospero says. "Mine would," Ariel answers, "were I human."[3] Something like that happens when a man sees the things of his life through the eyes of another. When he sees his world, his sexuality, his mortality through the eyes of another, they become human for

him. His affections become tender; he is able to consent to
them. When another human being comes between him and
the unknown, or when he himself as a child or a youth comes
between himself as a man and the unknown, he begins to become conscious of what has been happening to him. He
begins to realize that in spite of all its richness and strangeness it is something human, and he can say Yes to it.

The last thing of all to become human for him is his spirit
itself, his relationship to the things of his life. It is as though
his spirit could say, like Ariel, "were I human." It is his spirit
that goes through all the adventures of which we have been
speaking, from searching for a path of life to walking the
deadly clear path of death to being led on a path into the unknown, from gazing directly into the unknown to seeing it
lose its dread and fascination in a human eye. As his flesh begins to become human for him, to lose its dread and fascination and enter more consciously and willingly into his life, it
appears to him that a man of flesh has begun to rise in him to
challenge the man of spirit. Love and intimacy begin to enter
his life and they come into conflict with the life of his spirit
which has not yet become fully human for him. His struggle
with the unknown appears to him to have become a struggle
of flesh and spirit. In reality the conflict is within his spirit,
between seeing the flesh as human and not yet seeing itself
as human.

To realize that his spirit is human, that it is his relationship
to the things of his life, would be to realize that he is already
whole. He may come to sense his wholeness, to sense the
child within him and the youth still living on, their enthusiasms still alive, their eyes still there for him to see the world
in prospect. The old man may come to be there for him too,

before old age has come into his life, his eyes there already to see the world in retrospect. All the things of life are there, before they have entered and after they have passed. All are there because of his relationship to them, because of his spirit. It is the relationship, the spirit, that is the elusive thing. Somehow it remains inaccessible when he tries to approach it directly, when he goes into solitude and tries to come to grips with it.

Because his spirit is elusive, the things of his life become elusive too. Everything is there in him—the child, the youth, the man, and the old man—he is everything that a human being is, but he does not have access to it by himself. To gain access to what he is he must let others enter into his life, others who will evoke in him what he is, who will evoke the whole man in him. When another does enter into his life, he finds that he enters simultaneously into the other's life and that the other cannot call forth the whole man in him unless he gets in touch somehow with the whole human being in the other. The whole man lies deep within, like the drowned man of whom Ariel sings:

Full fathom five thy father lies . . .[4]

He lies at the depth of the spirit, "full fathom five" below the surface of life, and everything about him—the child, the youth, the man, and the old man—has been transformed by the spirit into "something rich and strange."

As it turns out, the drowned man of whom Ariel sings is not really drowned, his bones have not really become coral, his eyes have not really become pearls, his flesh has not really undergone a sea-change. All has been an illusion created by Ariel. The drowned man is really alive. The whole man of whom we have been speaking proves to be alive too when his spirit becomes human. When his spirit loses its inhuman aura, when it becomes consciously and willingly human, when it becomes for him simply his relationship to the things of his life, then the child in him, the youth, the man, and the old man all come alive.

The child is there living with the unknown in the moment, playing as time itself plays with all the things of life in their seasons. The youth is there living with the unknown in his life, facing the things that must enter into his life. The man is there living with the unknown in death, facing the things of his life that must pass. The old man is there living with the unknown in his spirit, facing the relationship he has established with the things of life in a lifetime of struggle. And the unknown is there wrestling with the child, the youth, the man, and the old man, wrestling like God with Jacob, until its dread and fascination have passed, always changing its shape like Proteus the Old Man of the Sea, until man becomes man and God becomes God.

# NOTES TO THE CONCLUSION

1. William Shakespeare, *The Tempest*, Act I, sc. 2, ll. 399ff. I am using the numbering in the Yale Shakespeare, *The Tempest*, ed. by David Horne (New Haven, Yale University Press, 1955).
2. Ibid., ll. 397f.
3. Shakespeare, op. cit., Act V, sc. 1, ll. 18ff.
4. Ibid., Act I, sc. 2, l. 396.